THE
WRITING
TRADE

• • • • • • • • • • • • • • • • •
VIKING

THE WRITING TRADE

A YEAR IN THE LIFE

JOHN JEROME

VIKING
Published by the Penguin Group
Viking Penguin, a division of Penguin Books USA Inc.,
375 Hudson Street, New York, New York 10014, U.S.A.
Penguin Books Ltd, 27 Wrights Lane,
London W8 5TZ, England
Penguin Books Australia Ltd, Ringwood,
Victoria, Australia
Penguin Books Canada Ltd, 10 Alcorn Avenue, Suite 300,
Toronto, Ontario, Canada M4V 3B2
Penguin Books (N.Z.) Ltd, 182–190 Wairau Road,
Auckland 10, New Zealand

Penguin Books Ltd, Registered Offices:
Harmondsworth, Middlesex, England

First published in 1992 by Viking Penguin,
a division of Penguin Books USA Inc.

1 2 3 4 5 6 7 8 9 10

Portions of this book first appeared in *The New England Monthly* in different form.

Page 256 constitutes an extension of this copyright page.

LIBRARY OF CONGRESS CATALOGING IN PUBLICATION DATA
Jerome, John.
The writing trade : a year in the life / by John Jerome.
p. cm.
ISBN 0-670-82885-8
1. Authorship. 2. Freelance journalism. 3. Jerome, John.
I. Title.
PN153.J47 1992
808'.02—dc20   91–16206

Printed in the United States of America
Set in New Baskerville
Designed by Ann Gold

•   •   •   •   •   •   •   •   •   •   •   •   •   •   •   •   •   •

This book takes place in but is not about 1989. That was the
year of Tiananmen Square, the freeing of Mandela, the removal of the Berlin Wall, the fall of Communism in eastern
Europe, the election of playwright Václav Havel as president
of Czechoslovakia. A book that was truly about 1989 would
concern those momentous matters, not one unknown writer's
daily struggles. This book is therefore a journal of a generic
year in the writing business.

C o n t e n t s

• • • • • • • • • • • • • • • • • •

THE
WRITING
TRADE

"He who talks doesn't know,
he who knows doesn't talk":
that is what Lao-tzu told us,
in a book of five thousand words.
If he was the one who knew,
how could he have been such a blabbermouth?
—Po Chü-i

• • • • • • • • • • • • • • • • • •

et's see, what's the best way to tell this? Spitting snow at dawn, forty degrees by noon. The eerie mildness of an open winter holds: yesterday, on New Year's Day, C. and I walked the forest loop in sneakers instead of January's more customary snowshoes. We survived Saturday night's obligatory New Year's Eve party by leaving early, and, yesterday, turned off the phone. Today, Monday, is the legal holiday, which we'll also observe. An essential truth of the freelance life: sure, your time is your own, but if you do business with the rest of the country, you do it when the rest of the country is working. You might as well take their holidays too.

No plans for today except one: to start this book, over which I have been rubbing my hands in anticipation for weeks now. So this morning I turned on the writing machine, formatted the page, entered the chapter title—and bailed out. Ended up answering mail instead, to avoid having to write down real,

1

allegedly permanent, words. Classic writer's fear of the blank page: call it tabula-rasa-phobia.

Okay, first of the year, inventory time. Here's where things stand. I've finished four of the sixteen essays for the next *Complete Runner's Day-by-Day Log and Calendar*, which I write every year. It isn't due until November 15, but I'll need to do a little better than one a month to finish up on time. Galleys for *Stone Work*, the book I completed last September, are scheduled to arrive in ten days, to be corrected and returned by the end of the month to get that book ready for publication in July. *The Sweet Spot in Time*, originally published in 1980, is being reissued this spring, but needs no attention from me until then. Whatever efforts I make on its behalf can't exactly be scheduled, but they'll take away writing time. I've also reluctantly signed up to write a couple of magazine pieces, the research for both of which must be done by March 1, the text finished by midsummer. It is not exactly a crowded calendar, except that I must at the same time proceed systematically with this book, in order to deliver it on schedule.

And what will such a year yield? Where will this assortment of tasks and obligations leave us? Moderately broke, for one thing. The scheduled activities will generate about two-thirds of a year's income, and we'll be scrambling, as usual, for the rest. Next May marks my thirtieth year as a professional writer, my twentieth as a freelance. Why haven't I learned how to make these years come out right?

The crunch is a little more severe than usual because of *Stone Work*, in which I have much too large an investment. I finished it a year late, subsidizing the extra year in part with an overstretched line of personal credit. That breaks every rule of freelance writing. (Don't do anything on spec, don't do anything that you can't finish on the up-front money, don't

depend in any way on actual sales, or expect any outcome
other than receipt of the final check for the agreed-upon
price.) I have too large a psychic investment as well: *Stone
Work* is an attempt to break out of the special-interest ghetto,
to stop writing category books. If it is well received I hope to
have less trouble interesting publishers in noncategory books
in the future; if it drops silently into the great abyss, as
happens with ninety-eight percent of the fifty thousand titles
that are published every year, I may be driven back to writing
about sports and pop science, for which my enthusiasm is no
longer high.

Stone Work is done, though, and it's this new project that I
dive into with a surge of relief. I've been without a book to
write for three months now, doing bits and pieces, finishing
up the business part of the writing year. I'm more than ready
to get back into the long, steady flow of real work, chasing
ideas down the page. Now, I think, I can begin to get some
rhythm back into my life.

This book is to be about writing, for which my credentials
are modest enough: a string of eight books that have ranged
from marginally successful to downright futile; a couple of
hundred magazine articles over all those years. I can't pretend
my work has ever done more than pay its (and my) own way.
I am a competent but essentially invisible writer, proof that
one can earn a living from writing for years without ever
breaking into the public consciousness. That's okay, or so I've
always claimed: all I ever wanted was to write, quietly, for a
living. Who knows what monstrosities of ambition lie buried
in that assertion?

The aim here is to show how a writing life works: a book
about the workaday process of making sentences for a living.
The plan—we'll see how well I'm able to follow it—is to focus

on the problems that arise in the writing, and their solutions. If I am distracted from that pure intention, it will probably be, as now, by money. Freelancing is an ongoing exercise in creative financing. When I was a salaried magazine writer I used to race automobiles and ski icy mountains, but I don't do those things anymore; there's adrenaline enough in meeting the monthly nut. There are other concerns in the freelancer's life, but with $801.27 in the bank at the first of the month, at the first of the year, and the mortgage due, I can't think what they are.

In that sense, then, this is going to be an adventure story. I just don't know yet what the adventure is going to be. The year could be anything from a rousing success to an unmitigated disaster; who knows what will get written during it, and about it? A scary thought, but the adventure metaphor puffs me up. I believe I'll think of myself as an explorer, mounting an expedition to get us to a very specific goal: solvency on January 1 of next year. Anything on top of that will be gravy.

· ·

A quarter inch of new snow last night, putting down a thin dusting in the woods: the dark brown points of fallen leaves curl up through the snow, making a speckled, polka-dotted forest floor. It is almost dizzying, and beautiful. If I saw it on film, my immediate thought would be, "Too bad they didn't get more snow." In a photograph I wouldn't see the woods for what they are, I would be trying to correct them, improve them. It is a habit I would like to break.

There's a wonderful moment in Woody Allen's *Radio Days*, when the narrator shows us his old Coney Island neighborhood. The shot is of a short residential street in a howling rainstorm, with windswept gray ocean in the background.

Squat three-story houses line the street, distressing in their ugliness. Then the voice-over says that the thing he always remembered about the old neighborhood was how beautiful it was, and the moment he says that, you realize it is true. Wonderful filmmaking, I think. Or wonderful writing, same thing.

Every day at noon I walk this loop. I am exercising the dogs, and taking a break, and trying to see—to learn to see —what in the woods is different and what is, reassuringly, the same. When work is going well the walk comes after a solid morning of progress, of watching problems arise and, slowly, tentatively, teasing out solutions to them. And then, if I have the patience, improving the solutions. When the work isn't going well, the walk brings, or is supposed to bring, temporary escape. Maybe I should start the book all over again today. Maybe I got misdirected yesterday because I started it before I'd started the year, which begins with this walk.

. .

Let me try again to set the scene, to say who is doing this and why. C. and I live in rural western Massachusetts, and work at home (which is the best part of the whole deal). C. is forty-five, I'm fifty-six; we are ex–magazine editors who fled New York in the mid-sixties, and have scrabbled together a living by writing and editing ever since. C. has her own editing business, working for various book publishers, and currently writes a column for *New England Monthly*. I write books (eagerly) and magazine pieces (only when I have to. for the money). I've also worked as an ad writer, have written speeches and documentary film scripts, but mostly I've been a journalist, covering automobile racing, skiing, and athletics. Those aggressively nonliterary subjects have paid my bills and allowed me to travel a good part of the world, but they have been passing entertainments. I've always been much more interested in writing than in any of the subjects I was writing about. I've always felt that any piece of writing is about writing first, before it is about whatever its subject matter is supposed to be. This time, no subterfuge: a book about writing a book.

Writing is a mysterious process even to writers—especially, perhaps, to writers. The debate over whether the skill can be taught has never been resolved. I can't tell how to do it, I can only tell how I do it, one way out of thousands. That I've never had time to think consciously about how it is done is one reason this project entices me so.

• •

What I'm trying to do here—this halting effort to set out the circumstances from which a book is supposed to emerge —is what some writers call establishment: imparting a sufficient amount of information to get the reader comfortable in the room, so to speak. I first heard the term in 1965, I think, from William Ziff, the eccentric publishing prodigy who would build Ziff-Davis Publishing Company into a half-billion-dollar empire, sell off the bulk of its many magazines, and then build a new stable of magazines approximately as large as the original.

I had worked for Ziff on a car magazine, quit to write advertising, then come back to the firm to join the staff at *Skiing*, which he had just acquired and which needed editorial help. He decided, for good and sufficient reasons, that I needed editing lessons, and for an uncomfortable few weeks I would go to his apartment on the Upper West Side each evening directly after work. While his wife prepared our dinner, he would quiz me about obscure Austrian ski racers and the fine points of ski technique, subjects about which I did not yet know a single thing. Often we would toss a football on his penthouse terrace while we talked; he seemed to need to do something with his hands. Or maybe he was checking out my motor coordination, to see if I could make a sufficiently skilled skier to work on his magazine.

We also spent those evenings tearing apart past issues of *Skiing* and several other magazines, analyzing every element, right down to typefaces on the masthead. Establishment was one of Ziff's fixations. By it he meant the scene-setting: a quick sense of what you're going to get, as a reader, if you read the piece. "Comfortable in the room" was Bill Ziff's phrase, I think, although I can't be sure I'm quoting him correctly. It was nearly twenty-five years ago.

If I learned anything about the sport of skiing from these sessions, it was how little I knew. I probably did learn a good deal about the making of magazines—to Bill Ziff's taste, anyway—but little of that sticks in my mind now. The other lesson that registered, that I still think about almost every day when I'm writing, came not out of skiing but surfing. There were magazines for that sport scattered throughout Ziff's living room. (I think he was considering the acquisition of one at the time.) Surfing writers, he pointed out, always told you what it was like to ride the surf at a given place in a given set of weather conditions. They didn't tell you what the area or the beach was like, they told you what the waves did, and where you had to go and what you had to do to get a good ride. The skiing magazines of the day never told you what it was like to ski down this trail or that one, and ski trails come in a great deal more variety than waves do. I would spend a good part of the next several years trying to get down on paper what it was like to ski particular mountains.

This, too, has to do with putting the reader in the room—on the wave, or the mountain—where the piece is taking place. A few years ago I started keeping a journal, and when I look back now at early entries, what interests me isn't what I was thinking about so much as what was going on with the weather: what it was like to be here, on this place, living this life, at that time.

• •

Furnace conked out in the middle of a below-zero night. The repairman got it going again about six, but the house wasn't fully warm by noon. I tried to work, but the cold, and something about getting up at three-thirty, militated against concentration, and I can't say I got a great deal done. Another bright, bitter, windy day, about ten degrees.

• •

On Sunday we asked Hans and Lynne over, bartering Bloody Marys for Hans's professional photographic talents: the publisher wants a book-jacket shot for *Stone Work*. I hate this process, but know that when I read a book, I enjoy having a sense of what the author looks like. I am a diffident and embarrassed subject, uncomfortable to the point of freezing when a camera lens points at me.

C. is worse. There's a wonderful photograph of her at about age eight, walking hand in hand down a dirt road with an elderly uncle. She's always hated the photo, and for years didn't know why. Her brother, a camera buff, had posed them, telling Uncle Ed to take C.'s hand. Ed complied. C. loved Ed dearly, but they did not have a handholding relationship. When he took her hand, she recognized that the business of photography had tricked him into violating some essential genuineness between them. When she finally figured it out, she says, she understood why primitive cultures say the camera captures your soul.

· ·

Galleys arrived this morning for both *Stone Work* and a little one-thousand-word piece I'd done for *New England Monthly*. I looked at the magazine piece quickly, in case a deadline was impending. The editors had made small changes—to my ear the piece now reads like the same song played on a piano that's slightly out of tune—but nothing worth arguing over. The organization was improved; maybe I'm not perfect after all. I'll keep my mouth shut.

The *Stone Work* galleys are another matter, demanding great care. They are a first glimpse of the text set in type, printed on long sheets of paper before division into pages. They also represent the last real chance to amend the text without considerable expense, and seeing a manuscript in type for the first time almost always seems to reveal glaring errors, in taste and tone if not in subject matter.

I read through the entire book-length set quickly, catching a few typos, suffering moderate gloom at my occasional lapses into preachiness and other self-indulgences. I'll cut those paragraphs the next time through. C., who proofreads professionally, volunteered to give the galleys a thorough reading, so I handed them over to her.

· ·

Half an inch of snow last night, so the woods are freckled again—a two-color world, silent except for water trickling down the hillside. Undistinguished; if we were in the city it would be a dull and depressing overcast day, but here it's beautiful as usual. Borrowed $2,100 from the bank this morning to pay taxes.

· ·

C. has caught a dozen or so more errors in the galleys, many of them overlooked at the copyediting stage, demonstrating clearly the difference between a writer who thinks he is being careful and an editor who really knows how to be careful.

So then I settled down for a slow and careful second reading of my own. In that process—despite my determination, as Melville put it, "to make each sentence show its passport"—I convinced myself that my excesses of taste and technique were justified, that the galleys read just fine and should be left alone. I mailed them back and have been regretting it ever since, worrying about these bombs of self-importance, lying there in the text, embarrassing me before the book is even bound. After all that work and care, the extra year of fiddling with the manuscript, it is still mannered and stiff and too controlled, too subconsciously writerly. How desperately I want to get hold of that aspect of my craft—or my brain—that makes me commit those same errors, over and over again, after all these years.

· ·

I am now, finally, beginning to get back into the real work of writing, which for me means getting a couple of paragraphs up on the computer screen and then working them over: massaging sentences, massaging ideas, trying to retain the ones that are worth saving and say them more effectively, batting down the distracting new ones that come along. Or comparing, assessing, trying the new ones, seeing if they work, making judgments between and among them. A new idea will come in the middle of a paragraph, making me flip forward

10

on the electronic screen, making notes ahead of myself. I get involved in developing the new thought, and that paragraph takes off on its own, spilling more new ideas. Eventually I stall, and go back to pick up the thread where I left off. It is almost entirely a game of working back and forth, up and down the page: ". . . we achieve, if we do achieve, in little sedentary stitches, as if we were making lace," said W. B. Yeats.

. .

Check from my agent by Fed Ex, advance money for the next *Log*, allowing us a deep breath—and repayment of the tax loan.

That was pleasant, but a larger joy this morning was reading C.'s proposal for an Adirondack book, already quite solid and clear in the current early draft. She's off to get it copied and into the hands of Dick Todd, the Houghton Mifflin editor who has encouraged her all along.

My mouth hangs open. C.'s intimates, myself included, have been agitating for years for her to write more, but except for a few magazine pieces she has resisted, preferring to edit. When *New England Monthly* was launched in 1984, she gave up freelancing to sign on as managing editor; four years later, a few months before she retired from that demanding job, she started writing a column, "In the Country." It has been very well received, and she's continued it as a freelance. She has talked about writing a book someday—probably a biography, as she is an accomplished researcher and loves the form—but that was always off in the hazy future.

Last September we visited the Adirondacks and something about that landscape clutched at her soul, and we went to the Adirondack Museum, where one of the canoes on exhibit grabbed it harder. She swept up what research materials she could, came home and began reading, made another trip to

. . . .

the museum, and she'd found her subject matter and her book. I expected, as the experienced writer, to shepherd her through several painful drafts of a proposal, helping her shape it, get the emphasis right, maybe even suggest a sentence or two. But except for a couple of dinner-table conversations, I haven't been involved. The thing's done, done well, and, barring some stupidity on the part of the publishing business, it should sell. In another month or two we should both be settled in and writing books. And I have a sneaking suspicion that hers is a better, more fruitful project than mine.

. .

I have wasted the productive part of the day on mail and bills, on the whining cloud of details that surround any business. I should handle these things in ways that would be less interruptive, but I don't. I have difficulty settling to work with nagging details hanging over me. I always think they'll take ten minutes, and end up spending half a day on them. I bring a great deal of fussiness to these concerns. Nobody ever said I was not neurotic.

I know perfectly well how to have a good writing day: get up around six, get a quick breakfast, at my desk before seven for an uninterrupted three hours of solid work (invariably the most productive segment of the day); a break at ten to fetch the mail, then back to work—resisting, by sheer strength of character, the seductions of the mail—until noon. Break again to walk the loop, get lunch, read the paper. Back to the desk for another productive couple of hours, until concentration inevitably fades; sag away from the desk about four, get a nap, feed and exercise the dogs, and begin, cocktail in hand, to read whatever it is I'm reading at the time. Piece of cake. I get a writing day like that, oh, at least once a month.

I'd have had a day like that today, but as I was dumping out the coffee grounds one of the little rubber bumpers fell off a cabinet door, and I wanted to replace it before it got lost. The glue on the back of the bumper had failed, but I had some two-sided tape that I'd bought for another project. I zipped upstairs and brought it down, applied it carefully, zipped back upstairs for the X-Acto knife to trim it to fit. Considered whether I shouldn't just redo the rest while I was at it. Made a quick count: forty-two cabinet doors, two bumpers per door. Decided I'd better get to work instead.

And so on: what that perfect schedule fails to accommodate are phone calls, trips downstairs every six minutes to let a dog in or out, keeping up with laundry, taxes, supplies, trying to find the quote in the book that could be shelved in any one of four rooms, over two floors. Devising new filing schemes so it won't take so long to find the quote next time. Inventing new organizations of research materials, ever more complex ways of losing all that valuable information I spent so much time gathering in the first place. In addition to being my own executive secretary, shipping clerk, and production manager, and, with C., pet groomer and trainer. And staying in contact with the kids, siblings, and friends, keeping the cars running and the house from falling apart, the larder filled, the skis waxed and the snowshoes varnished. Actually, I've been trying to put a note in here about a perfect writing day for the past week and a half, but I keep not finding the writing time.

· ·

This morning's diversion: digging out ten-year-old reviews of *Truck* for the publisher. It was my most successful book, and they'd like to pitch *Stone Work* as a sequel—which, in ways I'm not sure I can characterize, it is.

. .

C. finished her Adirondack proposal but it wasn't quite right, so she went browsing through her research, looking for some aspect of it that she'd left out, that would sharpen its appeal. The inspiration for the whole project was the *Sairy Gamp*, a canoe that weighed a mere ten and a half pounds. It was commissioned by an outdoor writer named George Washington Sears (who weighed only about a hundred and ten pounds himself) for a cruise through the Adirondacks in 1883. C.'s plan is to retrace that voyage, using it as narrative thread to examine the region, the park, the history, the man, and anything else that catches her fancy.

What she found in her notes, to introduce the subject, was a scene written by Sears himself, describing the arrival by rail of one of his earlier ultralight canoes. A crowd gathered: "They made comments on her unknown owner, and invariably ended with lifting her gently by the nose . . . [exclaiming] 'Holy Moses! Who's going to paddle *that* eggshell?' A clergyman said, 'I do declare, is that intended to go on the lakes?'

"None noticed the little gray-haired fellow who, dressed in coarse blue flannels, smoking a clay pipe, dangling his short legs off the platform and reading the latest number of *Forest and Stream*, was quietly taking in the thing—until the agent pointed him out as the Skipper of the little craft they were admiring."

In place, the scene works beautifully to introduce C.'s proposal: a simple bit of narrative, with some people in it, to get things rolling. I think of this as I find myself circling back to the Bill Ziff story. I must have thrown that in not so much because Ziff was critical to my education as a writer but, unconsciously, because I wanted a stronger narrative thread.

• •

Book-jacket photo mailed, along with a note to my agent listing magazines that might take an excerpt from *Stone Work*. With galleys on hand we can pursue these markets, and conceivably generate a little more income, not to mention valuable exposure for the book.

C. heard the chickadees' spring song this morning. Too damned early.

• •

Lunch with Bill MacLeish, who is fighting a rising panic about the promotion, or lack thereof, of his book, *The Gulf Stream*, scheduled for publication late next month. The book got a good review in *Kirkus*, a trade publication, but a review copy seems somehow not to have arrived at *Publishers Weekly*. These early brief reviews are generally regarded as helpful in convincing booksellers of a book's prospects. Bill was first told that the projected print order was thirty-five thousand, but when neither the chain stores nor the book clubs took the book, that figure was cut to fifteen thousand. Soon after that Bill's editor retired, so he no longer has a personal representative biting and scratching for him in the halls of his publisher. He's beginning to feel a bit abandoned, struggling to maintain his equanimity when the publishing business seems to be so bollixed up at the critical point of marketing. Someone, he says, should go straighten out the way the industry treats writers. But who has the time?

Nevertheless, he's nearly finished putting together an episode for *Nova*, based on his book, to air at publication time. That should help.

. . . .

· ·

Four inches of wet new snow, sleeting now; enough ice so I had to leave my car at the bottom of our long, steep driveway. But the woods are gorgeous, the hemlocks drooping with snow.

I took time off this morning to make some notes for the next *Runner's Log*. This requires getting my mind back into the tight little world of exercise physiology, a subject I've been writing about since the mid-seventies, and about which the chances of saying anything new seem to be dwindling rapidly. The *Log*, which I like to think of as my day job, is not exactly a book—fifteen monthly essays and an introduction, sprinkled through a glorified desk calendar—but it is my last remaining obligation (crosses self, knocks on wood) in the field of category books. Not writing category books is a great release to the imagination and productivity. But switching back into the categories for a few days each month is no bad deal.

I didn't know I was writing category books until I discovered where booksellers shelved *Truck*. That was supposed to be the tale of the disassembly and reassembly of an old pickup truck—my original intention had been to write a lighthearted essay on how automobiles actually work—but it turned out to be less about automobile mechanics and more about living in the extremely rural, extremely nontechnological northern end of New Hampshire. The chain stores chose to shelve it either among the Chilton Auto Repair Manuals or in the "Religious and Inspirational" section—along with *Zen and the Art of Motorcycle Maintenance*.

That was in 1977. Not long after, I read an interview with Joan Baez, whose new album had absolutely disappeared. It had been a new kind of music for her, not folk, not country-

and-western or rock-and-roll or easy listening or classical. Unfortunately, there were few radio stations left in the country that weren't formatted for one of those categories. With no radio stations to play the album, she said, it didn't get heard, didn't sell, and fell off the edge of the known universe.

This led me to the theory that there are only five categories of anything. Back in the sixties, when I was writing automobile advertising, some engineer calculated that since Chevrolet was offering forty-six models, thirty-two engines, twenty-one colors (and nine two-tone combinations), and more than four hundred accessories, the number of different cars that a Chevrolet customer could order was greater than the number of atoms in the universe. But every one of those umpteen zillion cars was one of five basic categories of car—I know, I was writing what we called the five-car ads, which portrayed the entire product line. If you wanted something, for example, that measured under twenty feet in length or weighed less than thirty-five hundred pounds, you were just about out of luck. Thus the great variety that computers were supposed to bring has evaporated on us. If the object of the game actually was to give us more choice, I suppose that computers could do it, but the object is to rationalize inventory, streamline manufacture and shipping, cut costs.

As the book chains now seem to operate, if they don't know which shelf a book goes on, they don't stock it. If the chains don't take it—see *The Gulf Stream*—the publisher prints fewer copies; if there are fewer copies printed, there won't be books available even if the book is well received. One irritating thing about all this is that when an occasional book does break through, creating a new category for a while, it drags a string of imitations along behind it, just like the movie sequel business.

• •

A gray day, forty-five degrees, crusty old snow two inches deep; as I walk I try to work my way into that peaceful state that lets me walk along and look at the woods without congratulating myself for walking along and looking at the woods. Without trying to write a picture of myself walking along looking at the woods.

Most of these notes are made during walks. I am not a great walker, not a prodigious walker. Virginia Woolf walked two hours a day, Thoreau four hours. I walk about thirty minutes. My loop is only a mile and a half, more valuable perhaps for its interruptive effect than as exercise. My labor is sedentary, and I figure I owe myself a break from it now and then: get up and move around a bit, just as people whose labors require them to move around all day owe themselves a chance to sit still now and then.

That's the rational view. What my daily walk really accomplishes is to force me to spend some time with the machines turned off (computer, phone, radio, record player, TV), with nobody talking and—most important—nothing I can get my hands on to read. It is thirty minutes a day during which I absolutely have to entertain myself. Thinking is the only entertainment available; what I end up thinking about is what I am working on. To think about that is almost always to drive it a little further forward.

I don't start out saying, Okay, now I have to work on the February *Log*. I try instead to pay attention to the woods, to take in the much realer outdoor world, but of course what happens is that I start working. Problems that have nagged at me during the morning come popping back into my head. Even if I am only explaining them to some nonexistent or imaginary companion (usually the absent C.), I do start putting them into sentences. The interior monologue—or droning babble—that is the raw material of writing starts up again.

Sometimes I think my goal in life is to be thinking about something else at the time.

· ·

Twenty-five years ago, riding the subway, a fellow magazine editor and I came across, as one will in New York, a disturbed citizen, raving about some injustice or other. "Letter to the editor," muttered my friend as we hurried past. There is an argument occasionally advanced by writers that writing is what keeps us sane. I'm not sure it's true. This is writing as exorcism, writing to rid oneself of some demon. I'm not sure it is the proper ritual. How sane is it to sit alone in a room, fashioning sentences, for as many hours a day as one can stand to sit there? And thereby lose complete contact with the very room you sit in, not to mention the world outside, the real world, your putative life? Maybe it is writing that keeps us crazy. Sometimes I think of coming out the other side: of shutting, finally, up.

Maybe writing keeps me crazy, and walking keeps me sane. The walking cure. Or perhaps walking would keep me sane if I didn't spend all my walking time writing. Our two dogs accompany me. I started walking for their benefit. (I wouldn't do it for myself.) Maybe it's actually the dogs that keep me sane. More nearly sane. "We'll be the judge of that," I imagine them saying.

· ·

C. is going through silent agonies, waiting for news on her proposal from editor Dick Todd (said news therefore referred to as The Word of Todd). I ran into him at the post office Saturday; he said he'd be in touch early in the week. We'll see.

· ·

Looking back at my story about Bill Ziff, I realize I neglected a physical description. Teachers always say you must put in the physical description of your characters. Give the reader a mental picture. I always forget. As a kid I skipped all description, perhaps because I never got around to looking up words like "aquiline."

Well, let's see. Ziff is a big, beefy, sleepy-faced guy, or was when I knew him, with the disconcerting habit of running his hands through his lank dark hair the wrong way, turning it into a momentary fright wig. He told me, with some amusement, that his wife checked each morning before he left for work to make sure his socks matched. She confirmed this, with matching amusement.

I'm a tall, skinny, old geek with short white hair and beard, see book jacket; C. is a lovely short woman, dark-headed, with silver eyes. Photographer Hans is tall, light, and handsome, a Dutch blond in his late thirties; his wife, Lynne, is a stunner in her early twenties, a young Ida Lupino. Dick Todd, mid-forties, is a sandy-haired, blue-eyed, red-faced Scot, always looking as if he's blushing or on the verge of blushing. MacLeish, known to loved ones as Willy, just turned sixty, is a tall barrel balanced on short parentheses, with a rim of gray-white beard and a very shiny head. Woody Allen is . . . oh, you know. Does this tell you anything?

"Directly you specify hair, age, etc., something frivolous, or irrelevant, gets into the book," says Virginia Woolf. I've been reading her memoir, in part for solace (considering the

tiny early sales of her books) and in part to get some idea of
what could be done with a writer's year. Books about writing
are an established genre and I should read everything in it,
but I am not going to. This isn't everything that's important
about writing, these are just the things that are important
to me.

• •

In the genre of writing about writing there is a tradition
of discussion of working methods, even to the physical layout
of the room and where the pencils are kept. In that tradition,
I should perhaps say that I work at a fairly rudimentary computer, hooked to an extremely rudimentary printer. The
printer is so slow that I sometimes stroll around the office
while I wait for it to finish a page. As I do, I'll spy a line as it
comes up on the page and see how to make it better, and
attempt to edit on the moving sheet of paper as it comes out,
my pen punching holes in the paper.

I do switch back and forth between the electronic and the
paper copy several times, finding that each change of medium
gives me a slightly fresher view of the writing thereon. It's a
useful way of breaking through the hypnosis of having mem-
orized one's own words. I mark up my manuscripts with a
fine-line red pen, making tiny little hen-scratch editorial
changes. A magazine editor once told me that he held a pencil
poised over any manuscript he read, and when his attention
began to fade, the pencil came down, drawing a vertical line
down the middle of the page, until his interest revived, at
which point he lifted the pencil. I do that for cuts, but when
I have trouble with the writing—and am too impatient to work
it all out at the moment—I just put a wavy vertical line in the
margin: fix this.

I fix what I can with the pen, and in the right frame of mind I'll go to some other room, a comfortable chair, a clipboard and a cup of tea, and make myself take a long, slow, leisurely trip through the manuscript, entering my changes as carefully as if the page were going next to a typesetter. That's the ideal. Usually, however, I can't make myself slow down that much, and after marking four or five pages I'll run into some problem too complex to be solved by hand, and rush back and pull the file up on the screen again so I can work on it there. It's so much faster. In the ideal situation I would go through the entire manuscript on paper, lavishly editing it, then put it aside for a week or ten days—or three months—before going back to make the electronic corrections. But the most productive method for me is definitely to keep going back and forth between paper and screen.

I know some one-draft writers, one of whom maintains that to spend another week on a manuscript neatening up the sentences is not going to make a hundred copies' difference in the number of books that are eventually sold, so why bother? I am unreconstructibly a multi-draft writer, a multi-*multi*-draft writer, and waste a lot of paper in the process. But I waste less now than in pre-electronic days: despite electronic writing's easy productivity and the sea of paper it seems to generate, I'd estimate that it saves me five or six reams a year.

Electronic writing allows the writer to send in a disk with his manuscript, therefore effectively typesetting his or her own books. I began doing that three books ago, thinking that I was saving my publishers money. When I dropped a joking hint that perhaps my next advance should include some recompense for all this labor I was saving them, I was told that there wasn't any saving. The printer raised his prices to make up for the lost business.

· ·

Something this morning put me thinking about the summer of 1952. I hadn't planned things right—a recurring problem, I notice—and needed a job in August, for the last month before going back to college. A local textbook publisher was hiring warehousemen, and I found it wryly satisfying, as a lit major, to apply. Nobody would hire a college kid for a single month, so I lied, saying I sought permanent work. My interviewer was a fussy little man wearing the first three-piece suit I'd ever seen. The job, he explained, was loading, stacking, and shipping cartons of books—hot, sweaty work in an un-air-conditioned warehouse. It needed a strong back and attention to detail. Fine, I said, just right, I'm your guy.

"But tell me," he said then, "are you a good writer?" I begged his pardon, unable to believe my ears. "How well do you write?" he asked.

My God, what was this? I was brought up not to toot my own horn, but this was a *publisher* speaking. When would I ever get another opening like this? When would someone ever even ask me that question again? I drew myself up, looked him straight in the eye. "It just so happens that I am a very good writer," I said as firmly as I could. "Some of my . . ." (teachers, I started to say, then remembered I wasn't supposed to be a college kid).

"Good," he interrupted. "A lot of the boys back there can't write their own names so you can read them. Shipping labels come through, we can't even tell where the cartons are supposed to go."

Writing is easy. All you have to do is cross out the wrong words.
　　　　　　　　　　　　　　—Mark Twain

· · · · · · · · · · · · · · · · · · · ·

*W*e're in a freakish warm spell, nearly sixty degrees with soft southern breezes; I'm out early to take advantage, walking the loop in sweatshirt and sneakers, enjoying a small tingle of freedom at going outdoors in February dressed so lightly.

Paid bills and worked on the February *Runner's Log.*

· ·

There's an almost osmotic awareness that I've gained from walking the loop so often: I now recognize the signatures of rot in the limbs that drop in the path, in the trees that fall. I see the disease on the bark, in the wood. I don't look for it, I just know that's what it is. Oh, yes, rotten wood. That's why it's down.

A botanist once pointed out to C. the sizable colonies of living things that collect around fallen trees, how the punky wood holds moisture so great numbers of species can survive there. I've been worrying about getting a coat of preservative on our deck—but what arrogance it is for us to think we can preserve wood (particularly in New England). We build things and then try to keep the "rot" out of them, which rot is actually life. What goes on with lumber is that life gets into it. We call it dead wood when it's rotten; what it is is wood that has more life in it: wood as medium for the collection of life.

. .

A phone call this morning from my editor, Amanda Vaill, resolving a couple of small typographical mysteries in the galleys of *Stone Work*. Down the hall, she says, reaction to the book is beginning to build. The psychologists—and my writer's paranoia—call this "confirmation bias." Once the publisher has decided to publish a book, those whose job it is to sell it must begin convincing each other that it's a fine one. To do otherwise would be too depressing. The same thing happens in writing: by the tenth time I've rewritten a page, my proofreading is aimed not at seeing how to make it better but at confirming to myself that it's really all right the way it stands.

. .

Spent the morning fixing the *Log* I started yesterday. Each of these is a six-hundred-word essay. When C. was working at *NEM*, she once asked John Skow for a six-hundred-word piece. "Let's see," Skow said, "six hundred words, that's about an idea and a half, isn't it?" When she told me this story, I was enchanted; I hadn't realized it before, but he's right. Each essay for the *Log* is an idea and a half. If I don't have the other half of an idea, I grind to a halt a little short of six hundred words. More frequently I try to cram two ideas into one essay and the piece goes off on a tangent, causing me a pesky struggle before it gets back under control. When something is wrong, it is almost always because I've tried to cram too many ideas into it.

I keep a "futures" file of ideas for these essays. To start a new one I pick a small idea out of the file, flip it onto the screen, and then develop it as far as it'll go. Yesterday's, predictably, was about half an idea short; today as I walked the loop I came up with the other half.

Sometimes the half-idea comes first, then develops into the real subject of the essay; sometimes the half-idea comes afterward, after I've run out of anything substantive to say and am groping for some comic turn or other device to finish the piece. This is definitely writing to fill, and thus a violation of the creative spirit; that preciousness aside, it can be fun to do. One of the most entertaining little chores in magazine work is writing picture captions. The art director gives you a "spec," something like three lines at thirty-six characters; you set your margins to that width and write three lines that describe the photo, but also attempt to slip in an intelligent comment, a mild joke, or some other element to engage the reader. It is more like working a crossword puzzle than writing, but it's an amusing challenge.

More of the writing business falls into this kind of hairsplitting than nonwriters might think. The most extreme version I know was for one of those automated billboards that keep spelling out new messages. It overlooked a crowded Detroit freeway, and on it a friend of mine attempted to sell Pontiacs to the drivers creeping along below. Unfortunately, the message space was fifteen letters long, and the client preferred that the word "Pontiac" should appear in it most of the time. The other eight letters were at my friend's disposal, to fill with anything witty or entertaining he wanted to say—so

. . . .

long as it kept selling hard, and the words "new" and "now" came up every other time or so.

The masters are seldom precious about such matters. According to one story, when *Ulysses* was first set in type the last page had only a few words on it, making for an awkward-looking product. The printer had the effrontery to ask Joyce if he would like to cut a line or two of his masterpiece; Joyce preferred to add, and cheerfully came up with a few more immortal lines to make the page look better.

• •

Whatever C. and I happen to talk about at dinner usually works its way into my notes the next day, and thence into this manuscript. It's as if one night's dinner sets the next morning's agenda; each evening is a chance for us to roll around on our tongues what we've done that day, and where we're headed next. We discuss these things, throw ideas at each other, brainstorm over each other's work. The next day we refine what we talked about the night before.

All of this is in further pursuit of the good working day. Jimmy Breslin once said that the job is to write three pages each day, and the next day try to save two of them. This is one of those neat lines that don't quite work out: save the two and you still have to add three to that, which really means writing five pages a day—which is a high rate of productivity.

It depends on what you're writing, of course. Magazine writing sometimes flows along at a thousand words a day—but writing for magazines generally requires two or three times more (or more intensive) research than writing books. That means two or three days of scut work for every day of writing: more like four days for a thousand words of production.

There are people who turn out high-quality newspaper

columns, nine hundred to twelve hundred words, three days a week. My hat is off to them: what looks dead easy is more than a full-time job. At one time I was writing three monthly magazine columns, but after thirty-six columns in one year my tongue was hanging out, and I was completely out of ideas. Many professional writers write a column on the side while they pursue their real work. It looks to be a dream setup, but turns out to be more of a stretch than they thought when they signed up.

In the matter of the good writing day, the real question is not how much work you can do but how much effective work, which is the problem that Breslin's formula addresses. Some years ago, for a column in *Esquire,* John Gregory Dunne traced the history of his most recent novel, over five or six years and several complete drafts. When he finally published the book, its length divided by his working time came out to almost exactly two hundred and fifty words per day.

• •

Bitter-cold night, ten degrees at noon, snow forecast for tomorrow. I finally remembered to get off a note to the publisher telling them that a thousand-word excerpt from *Stone Work* was previously sold to a magazine. Also, the contract for this book arrived, was signed, and put back in the mail: this manuscript is therefore officially under contract. I make note of that out of curiosity, to see how long it takes for the advance check—due upon signing—to get here.

• •

An inch and a half of new snow, not enough to bring out the snowshoes, which is what I'm waiting for in order to start the New Hampshire piece. Last fall I proposed to *New England*

Monthly that I do a winter piece about the Kinsman Ridge in northern New Hampshire, a fifteen-mile strip of mountains next to which C. and I used to live. My plan was to go up and snowshoe the familiar trails, visit old friends, write a piece that tried to get down in some kind of entertaining fashion the geology and geography, the climate and what it's like to live there, and everything else I could think of: a piece about place.

Dick Todd, the Houghton Mifflin editor who is considering C.'s Adirondack book proposal, is also editorial director of *NEM*. He and I went out for my first writer-editor lunch in years. I had a fairly complex rationale prepared, but when I said I'd like to do a piece about this little string of mountains where I used to live in New Hampshire, he said, "Fine," and that was pretty much the end of the discussion. He'd take a four-thousand-word piece—on the long side, as feature articles go. He particularly liked the idea of doing it on snowshoes, being an enthusiastic snowshoer himself. I've been waiting for the woods to fill up with snow ever since. (The snowshoes I gave C. for Christmas have so far never been strapped on anyone's feet.)

With bare ground still showing here, I'm beginning to fear we may run out of winter. Anyway, it's time to start planning. Hans will be doing the photography, so with Lynne we'll make up a foursome for the trip. Best idea of all: the house we used to own, in the little town of Easton, now belongs to a downstate couple who use it for ski weekends. If we can clear a date, they've offered us the use of our old house, which C. and I lived in longer than either of us had ever lived in a single location. That house is home, in some as yet unfathomed sense: I can't (yet) say why, but it has haunted my dreams during the ten years since we moved away.

. . . .

• •

Dick Todd is becoming something of a fixture in this narrative. He is former executive editor of *Atlantic Monthly*, who left that magazine at its last change of ownership for a rural life. He has taught writing in nearby colleges and done some freelance writing, and was drawn slowly into *NEM*. He has been a force for literacy and wit at that magazine, a valuable counterbalance to its sometimes more market-oriented sensibilities. C. found him a perfect gem to work with on magazine matters, which is why she's eager to have him as editor of her book.

I've never seen him in a short-sleeved shirt, even in hottest summer—which may explain his customary redness of face. One senses a certain reverence, in Todd, for the concept of shabby-genteel; he writes *NEM*'s Manners column, and brings to it an acerbic quality that is startling, considering its seemingly gentle source. In the beginning he used a pen name in the magazine, for no reason that he would articulate to me. (He told C. he didn't want his writers to feel he was competing with them.) He is in fact a more graceful and intelligent writer than just about anyone I know, but he must spread his large talents between editing books and editing magazines—and teaching, and a little writing—while three teenage daughters go thundering into their expensive college years.

• •

Spent the morning gathering stuff for the IRS, irritated once more at the financial details of our lives. But out on the loop, with the sun breaking through snow-covered hemlocks, it is possible to regain some measure of serenity. I stop at the edge of the frozen pond to examine the scene, and fluffy, almost Caribbean clouds are whisking across the sky from west to east. An enormous amount of energy is boiling away in the atmosphere today. Being a freelance writer is not such a bad deal.

I said just that to a physician once. I'd gone to a new doctor; after he'd taken my medical history, he asked me briefly about my life situation. "Oh, it's great—I'm a freelance, I work at home at stuff I really like," I said. "I have a wonderful deal." He jotted something down on my file, and stood to escort me into the examining room. I couldn't resist a surreptitious glance at the file he'd left open on his desk: "Has wonderful deal," he'd written, and drawn a circle around the words. It's an incident I try to remember around tax time.

. .

We're scheduled to go to the Caribbean next month—on tickets paid for last summer—and the place is on my mind. Now I get a letter from my son, Marty, a magazine editor, just back from his first visit: "Information is a refreshingly soft thing to the natives. The police gave fuzzy or incorrect street directions when we asked. Vendors who'd sold fruit or fish for twenty years rarely knew the specific names of their goods. I became self-conscious at my nervous Western need to attach a name to something, as if knowing I was eating a flying fish or a king fish somehow made it sanitary or delicious. Ask a vendor the name of a fruit, and he would likely shrug at the silly formality of calling it anything more specific than 'fruit.' Instead, a machete would come down, slicing it in half for us to taste."

I had struggled for pages to say something like that in *Stone Work*—about the naming of things—and didn't get it down half so well. Now, I tell him, I want to steal his story about

31

the machete and the fruit, pry open the galleys, and insert it in place of my own clumsiness.

. .

Today is my brother Jud's sixty-second birthday; tomorrow would have been my mother's eighty-second. What an astonishing number of years have accumulated around our lives. I got into the writing business in the first place because, thirty-four years ago, I bought a Volkswagen and joined the West Texas Sports Car Club. The club wanted a newsletter; I was teaching high school, and, having access to the mimeograph machine in those pre-Xerox days, I became its editor and publisher. Wrote it, typed it, ran it off, stapled and stamped it, mailed it; three-cent stamps, as I recall.

After a number of issues a fellow member in the insurance business suggested expanding the newsletter into a commercial search-and-find source for scarce foreign-car parts. I quit teaching to become a publishing mogul. The publication was to consist entirely of classified listings, but we never got the bugs worked out of the parts-search notion, and I couldn't resist putting in an occasional joke anyway: it gradually turned into *Sports Car Digest,* a newspaper about racing. We found an oilman with a sense of humor to back it for three totally profitless years, after which he found a better investment (named Billy Sol Estes). So we folded the paper, and I got a job in Denver as a technical writer in the missile business. I was hired not because of any demonstrable skill at writing but because I was born in Tulsa: an opening occurred in a section headed by a man who happened to be from that town.

. .

Bitter, bitter cold, seventeen degrees and forty-mile-per-hour winds. Getting around the loop is a test of character for me, a fresh-air stroll for the goddamn dogs.

. .

This morning I found out that *Staying Supple* is out of stock and Bantam does not intend to reprint. This was a how-to book about maintaining athletic flexibility that I wrote two years ago. A chiropractor who had sold a couple of hundred copies to his patients called to ask about getting more books. "Out of stock, do not reorder," came the message.

After the shock wore off, I remembered that my agent had told me that to stay alive in the "New Age" category, in which Bantam had placed the book, it would need to sell twenty thousand copies per year. Bantam ordered a first printing of only 12,500 copies, probably on the basis of orders from booksellers (which meant that the book was effectively dead before publication date—although I certainly didn't understand that at the time). The copies that were printed lasted eighteen months; now, therefore, it is out of print. Meanwhile I'm getting calls from phys ed teachers who want to use the book as a text. Don't ask *me* what's wrong with the publishing business.

As Bantam has let it die, the rights revert to me. My assumption is that we'll be able to find a smaller publisher, interested in acquiring rights to a book that sells eight thousand per year and might continue to do so for a long time, which is the kind of book *Staying Supple* was designed to be. If that happens, the only loss will be any momentum that Bantam's promotional efforts (and my own) might have built up.

. .

A little nervous news about the New Hampshire piece: *NEM* is in the process of changing hands, and is temporarily out of cash. I know this only because of C.'s long-standing connection with the magazine, but there's a legitimate worry that if the deal falls through, Hans and I might never get paid for the New Hampshire piece. We decide to make the trip anyway, as a brief winter vacation, but to keep our investment minimal until the financial situation comes clear.

. .

Spent the morning attempting to rescue *Staying Supple*, notifying people I know will want more copies, telling them they should make their needs known to Bantam. It won't work, but I'd feel like a quitter if I didn't make the effort. I even began having a little fantasy about getting the rights myself and self-publishing it, or getting some small-time entrepreneur to take it over. But that, I keep reminding myself, is not a smart way to spend my time.

. .

I tried to write fiction in college, the usual bad short stories. I tried to write afterward but had nothing to write about, spent hours staring at the typewriter, wishing I were writing. Automobiles gave me the first subject matter that got me out of my own cramped and airless head. I did manage to sell one short story during the *Sports Car Digest* days, but figured that was a fluke—although I welcomed the three hundred dollars it paid, half a month's salary. I kept trying to write fiction after moving to Denver, and one day my wife called me at work to tell me I'd received another check for three hundred dollars

—payment for a second short story that had somehow arrived ahead of news of its acceptance.

This sale, I decided, meant that earning a living from writing might be possible. At five o'clock I drifted out of the missile plant and drove slowly home, dreaming about what that might mean. I might be able to live anywhere I wanted to, might not even have to have a regular job. I was so lost in thought that I couldn't remember whether I'd picked up my regular passenger, couldn't remember leaving her off at her house, couldn't remember what route I'd taken. I had to phone to make sure she'd gotten home okay. I never sold another short story.

Sports Car Digest had attracted some attention in the automotive press, and shortly thereafter *Car and Driver* plucked me out of Denver and moved me to New York as an associate editor. I was given a desk, a typewriter, and a first assignment, a badly written article about a British racing track. Fix it, I was told. I panicked.

Then I remembered my first fiction sale. The story had been rejected, but with a note on which the editor had scrawled, "Show 'em, don't tell 'em." Well, hell, everybody knew that; if that's what they wanted, I thought as I rolled up my sleeves, stand back. I rewrote my story, changing description to action and action to dialogue. I pulled out all the stops, every trick I could think of, felt I was turning it into the corniest and most overdramatic piece of self-satirizing crap ever written, and sent it off. Back came a check.

That memory returned as I stared at the piece that *Car and Driver* told me to fix. Okay, the hell with it, I said to myself again, and plunged into the rewrite. I just tried to make it read well; it went directly into type, and was printed. I never looked back.

For one of her early magazine columns, C. was having start-up problems, walking around it, unable to write for a day or two. Then suddenly she had it done, and that night I asked her how she'd gotten going. "Well, I spent the usual time convincing myself I couldn't do it," she said, "and then I finally realized I had a couple of things to say about this subject, and wrote those down, and then I was going." Exactly, I thought. Ask yourself what you have to say, put it into a readable English sentence, repeat the process. Make a joke or two, string some ideas down the page. It isn't so hard.

• •

A paragraph from today's notes, transcribed directly:

> By this point the obsessiveness of detail about the business side of writing may well be merely exasperating. Part of this is a deliberate exercise in tripping around the edges of the real subject (the act of writing)—and part of it is fear: that to write about the writing process itself is to drag to a stop in self-consciousness. It isn't self-consciousness I fear—that's one of the things I want to explore—but loss of momentum. Consider how one might write about writing: do the sentence as it is first thrown down, before it gets fixed, and then analyze what's wrong with it; spell out the suggested fixes and their various failures, the examples of repairs, the twisting details of the small decisions that are made, some of them pointless and some not so. Sounds to me as if it'd bog down completely.

The paragraph doesn't make much sense as it sits, but there are some things in it that I want to get at. How to make them intelligible? One problem I see is that I've thrown three subjects into one paragraph: the accumulation of detail about the business side, the self-consciousness of writing about writing itself, and the problem of writing about technique.

The accumulation of business detail started almost as a joke: who could possibly be interested in these grocery receipts of an unknown writer? The joke may have gotten away from me, however. I am reminded of William F. Buckley's *Cruising Speed,* which started out as a picture of a busy writer-celebrity's whirlwind life and ended up a self-parodic paroxysm of name-dropping.

Maybe I ought to make clear that this year is relatively uncluttered with business, and if that part seems to get in the way of writing time for the likes of me, imagine how it must be for a successful author, with a real body of work out there and a constant string of business details to deal with.

The question of self-consciousness is a larger matter, almost a philosophical one: can a book about writing a book even be readable? As it happens I've been reading John Updike's memoir with that very title—*Self-Consciousness*—although he's talking about another kind, the awkward self-involvement of a shy and uncomfortable man. The self-consciousness I'm worried about is the deliberate violation of what might be called the writer's proscenium arch, which spans the top of this very page. One implied task of the writer is to sweep readers into forgetfulness: to make the writing disappear, in effect; to make you forget you're in the act of reading.

My problem with this implied covenant is that it pulls the writer into a basic dishonesty—so what I'm doing here is violating it: not bothering to disguise the fact that there's an unsure and oftentimes dull-witted human being on the other side of the writing machine. This entails an unusual degree of honesty, and I'm working at that. It's hard, after all these years of hiding behind writerly tricks.

The specific techniques of working on a piece of writing are another matter—and mostly have to do with the fixing of sentences. I throw the sentence up onto the screen any old way, getting down some semblance of the idea, if just as a hint to myself. Then I start working it into shape, trying to make it convey the idea as effectively as possible. Or, more accurately, I try to make it *say* the idea: try to rescue it from the vague state in which it emerged from my head. Writing is a process of going over and over the material endlessly, getting what you're trying to say driven into a corner.

I may make a conscious attempt to analyze what's wrong with it. I may try to figure out which words are the most important, whether there are more vivid or more accurate words to put in their place, where in the sentence they will strike most effectively. I will invert the sentence, move it elsewhere in the paragraph, try to set it up more efficiently or pay it off more dramatically. But mostly I just keep moving elements around, looking for the meaning to come clearer. Before the days of electronic writing I would cheerfully retype a page to reverse two elements in a sentence, then decide that the new version was less effective than the old, and type the page once again to move them back to their original position.

The reason this tedious process isn't boring to do is that each successful change reveals a little something you didn't yet know about what you're trying to get said. When you finally get the sentence to pop clear, there's a sense of fulfillment, of closure, of having gained the idea. It is the feeling of having gained a new understanding, I think, that keeps us reading as well as writing.

Writing about writing usually ends up saying that the product is something that bubbles up out of the unconscious. The writer's task is to gain access to the unconscious, find its surprises, let its surprises come out. This sounds extraordinarily pat but is probably true. It is usually invoked to explain fiction and poetry, but needn't be restricted to the wilder shores of writing. Ideas, large and small, come bubbling up from some hidden spring and emerge—for me, anyway—on the edge of coherence. Forcing them over into accessibility may take conscious thought, hard analysis, and all those other left-brain modes of working. We make plenty of conscious decisions about the things we write about, but the things themselves come up out of some other well.

This line of thought reminds me, with embarrassment, of those times as a younger writer when a sentence would suddenly appear on the page that I had no real intention of saying, but that was expressed so dramatically that I would accept and attempt to defend the position it staked out. High-school ideology is born this way; it's the scary version of not knowing what you think about something until you begin writing about it. Sometimes you have to have the courage—or energy—not to say something you've just said, or think you've said, terribly well.

• •

This afternoon is Willy's book-signing, at World Eye, a nice bookstore in Greenfield. C. and I will attend. Willy is known in town, and his book-signing should go well.

Some of them don't. In 1978 my mother talked a local bookseller (*the* local bookseller) in New Braunfels, Texas, into putting on a signing party for *Truck*. I'd gone to high school there, local boy writes book, etc. Unfortunately I'd left New Braunfels as soon as I could, never intending to go back—as had my high-school friends, both of them. I sat in a deserted bookstore for three hours and sold two copies of the book, one to my mother, the second to the cousin she dragged along with her. I had the feeling that my presence, advertised in the local paper, was actually keeping people out of the poor bookseller's store.

Book-signings work if you're Muhammad Ali or otherwise have a name; if you're not, you'll have to beat the bushes yourself. Of course celebrities pull people who don't otherwise buy books. I don't think I'm interested in drawing people who don't read books, since I think of myself as a book writer. But an editor once told me that if I want to sell books in large numbers, I'll have to sell them to people who don't ordinarily buy books. There aren't enough people who read books to support the people who write books. Something is wrong with this equation.

· ·

The loop trail is glare ice, but there are fallen leaves alongside, washed free of snow by last night's rain, that give decent footing. This is our tenth winter in Massachusetts, and completely different from all the rest. How many different kinds of New England winter can there possibly be?

Willy's signing was well done, nicely laid on, sold quite a few books. Good for his spirits. We go to New Hampshire tomorrow.

· ·

Home from the weekend in New Hampshire, uneventful but not unemotional. The first fifteen minutes or so in our old house had me absolutely transfixed, suffused with the warmth and sweetness of memory. It is a hundred-and-fifty-year-old ramshackle New England add-on, and the new owners have done a lot of sensible remodeling, but the parts that moved me were the bad patches, where it had always been particularly grubby and hadn't yet been fixed up. It is startling now to think how broke we always were when we lived there.

Hans and I walked up to Bald Knob, a couple of miles in ten-degree sunshine, on three inches of slippery snow over ice. There should've been three feet of snow; this bizarre winter holds even there. I was trying to find a spot that would show Hans, as photographer, what the place was like, something I could point him at and say, There, get that. Otherwise, what we mostly did was a kind of pointless driving around. I did not make any notes or do any other specific work on the magazine piece. Couldn't; too distracted by having another couple along. I'll have to depend on memory—and a later, solo trip.

But it was also good to make the trip with Hans and Lynne, because everything we saw had a story to it that they didn't yet know, that, in the telling, could begin to be shaped. It made me realize how anecdotal this piece can be: the places where we fetched Christmas trees in winter or raspberries in summer, where we slid off winter roads and got stuck, the swimming holes and picnic sites, the houses where friends' romances took hold or fell apart. I am confident that I could go up and down that valley and remember some kind of wry or funny story about nearly every house in it. If I can't, C. can. The social history of the valley's last couple of decades had mostly to do with the obdurate, conservative, preternaturally wary native population, dealing with, and eventually accommodating, the hippie influx—the city kids who fled there in the late sixties and early seventies.

It did occur to me, looking at those houses up and down the valley, that everybody who lived there wanted to be there. Almost nobody, except the occasional ski instructor, was pulled there by a job. The desire to reside in that particular piece of geography overcame the harsh climate, the economic uncertainty, the lack of facilities and services. You had to have a strong reason for being there—and there is no stronger one, I suppose, than just to be entirely in love with the land. The people who live there might not admit this, but when I look back on what I know of them, that seems to me to be the essential truth of the place.

Maybe that's the last line in the piece.

· ·

Todd finally told C. that the early, unofficial Houghton Mifflin response to her Adirondack proposal ranged from enthusiastic to lukewarm, but there may not be as much advance money as she needs to do the book. He suggested that she consider an agent, who can get it out in simultaneous submission to several other publishers, to see if she can find more support. If she does send it around, Todd still wants to be high on the list.

So she sent it to her first choice of agents and now awaits a response. She's also applying for a month's residency at an Adirondack writers' colony, which will be a great help in reducing research expenses.

· ·

I've been reading Ian Frazier's wonderful *New Yorker* piece on the Great Plains, and thinking what a nightmare it must have been for that magazine's legendary fact-checkers. Fact-checking has become something of an obsessive process on current magazines, and is one of the pestiferous reasons I do little magazine writing anymore. It's not that I want to print lies; it's that the fact-checkers and I don't seem to agree on what a fact is. I don't mind documenting my work, particularly anything that's legally actionable or otherwise risky, but when I have to spend extra hours explaining that my jokes are not actually researchable, and that I happen to have an opinion now and then, I get impatient. The fact-checking process instantly makes the editor-writer relationship an adversarial one. There are sufficient adversaries in the world without taking on editors.

It is my serious intention to do the New Hampshire piece as a nightmare for *NEM*'s fact-checkers, but to qualify everything so they not only won't be able to check anything but won't have to. I plan to talk strictly nice about the public lives of people in that valley, but to imply the undertone of mischief and high good humor and amused scandal (as opposed to horrifying dark deeds) that often seemed to ripple around the edges of those lives.

I don't want a bunch of twenty-year-old magazine interns phoning eighty-year-old friends who are not all that comfortable with telephones in the first place, to ask them if they really said thus and such in 1968. I'll write around the problem.

. .

Bluebirds on the fence at six-thirty this morning, a full month earlier than we've ever seen them before.

. .

Thinking about the New Hampshire piece this morning, a line came floating up from *On Mountains*, a book I wrote ten years ago: "Gradient is the elixir of youth." It refers to streambeds and erosion, the inevitable reduction to gentleness in geologic time, but the metaphor seems apt. New Hampshire mountain towns tend to be inhabited by old folks and young folks but not too many in between. People flee that harshness in middle age; some—the bolder, perhaps—return in later life. I'm not sure this generalization will stand up, but it feels right.

Hans and Lynne hadn't been to our particular part of the mountains, and we played a trick on them on the drive up. We'd taken two cars, since we needed to come home by separate routes. C. and I led them by a back road into Sugar Hill, so they didn't see a single mountain until we came over a ridge and were suddenly looking down into the Easton Valley, with the abrupt wall of Kinsman, Cannon, and Lafayette mountains—4,400, 3,800, and 5,200 feet, respectively—popping up on the other side. It's one of the most spectacular views anywhere in the White Mountains, and you have no hint that it's coming. We turned a corner and there the mountains were, freshly snow-capped on a perfectly clear blue-sky day, about three in the afternoon, nicely lit by the rapidly approaching February sunset: as dramatic a view as you could possibly get. The joke worked; they slammed on the brakes and were out of their car almost before it stopped rolling, Lynne with a rodeo yell, Hans clicking away with his cameras, his mouth open.

Our old house sits at the foot of Kinsman, a broad, gentle, classic triangle of a peak, named for Nathan Kinsman, an early settler. One thing C. and I had forgotten about living there was how much time we spent looking up at Kinsman, how conscious of that mountain we always were. My study looked out at it, and it was there outside my window while I wrote *On Mountains;* one chapter of that book, "Field Notes," describes a hike to its peak.

C. says now that she was startled on this return visit at Kinsman's dimensionality. She'd remembered it as a flat plane in the background to the east, but it has considerable depth to it, shoulders and humps poking out toward the valley, cirques and gulleys, slides. (Virtually every mountain in New England has at least one "Slide Brook" on it.) I have to find a way to talk about Kinsman that expands the possibilities of how one speaks of mountains. It looms in my mind as the eastern mountain of choice, the mountain by which all others are measured, at least for sheer benignity. By the topo map, our house was at about 1,100 feet, the peak above us 4,275: we were looking out on three thousand feet of relief. And somehow that's what I felt, what I still feel when I see it now: relief.

· ·

For the magazine piece I should also note how purely cold it was in that valley on that February weekend. It was one of the stranger things about the visit: how easily the temperature dropped to seventeen below at night, and how hard it struggled to reach ten above during the day. Saturday seemed like an ordinary day, only a few degrees colder than the day before in Massachusetts, two hundred miles south. We bundled up and went ahead with whatever we'd planned, but there was a pervasive ache, a thin intractability to the very air. Ten above seemed colder there than at home. You think you can step outdoors without a parka and do two quick things—get something out of the car, dump the garbage, whatever—but before you can get the second thing done, you notice you are in sharp pain. How quickly it turns from a discomfiting chill to pain. Hans's cameras regularly froze up and had to be tucked inside parkas for a few minutes to resume operation.

· ·

The first third of the advance for this book arrived this morning, a three-week turnaround. Pretty good for the publishing business.

· · · · · · · · · · · · · · · ·

· ·

C.'s would-be agent didn't much like the proposal. She seems to think C. should dump much of the history and turn it into a solo adventure story, how she canoed the Adirondacks and found God or something. C. is not inclined to change the emphasis to personal dramatics.

She described her quandary to Todd, who said she shouldn't rewrite the proposal on the basis of one agent's reaction. She can send it around on her own, to other publishers, he says, and get further reactions; it's a quirky book, and needs to find an editor who *gets* quirky books and can develop them. C.'s decision is to investigate a bit further how the agent thinks the book must be made to work, then decide how much she wants to revise the proposal—and whether she even wants to pursue working with that agent, or any agent.

· ·

My agent is Georges Borchardt, a sharp-witted Frenchman about whose personal life I know nothing except that at a tender age he somehow found himself in the Tennessee National Guard. Something about the Korean War and citizenship, I think. A friend of mine tells me he mentioned Georges's name to an editor once, who winced. "Borchardt," the editor said, "has a genius for beginning a negotiation at precisely the figure you planned as your last, desperate, final offer."

As an in-joke, C. and I once decorated a guest bathroom wall with rejection slips. We had a dozen or so in our files, but had been throwing them away for years, and wanted more samples. The next time I talked to Georges, I told him about our little project In the case of future rejections, I said, would he send me the originals? "Well, all right," he said in his

46

elegant French accent, "but then what will I hang on *my* bathroom walls?"

· ·

An inch and a half of snow last night—not the moisture we need, but it certainly helps the looks of things. There's a certain somberness to having Novemberish woods all winter long. It wears on you; a little white on the ground puts back some gaiety. This was a very fine snow, a granulated-sugar effect; the beauty is in the fine detail, the small breaks in the surface, the animal tracks and leaves and grasses, the yellow-on-white color scheme from weeds poking through.

Walking with Hans through the frozen woods on the flanks of Kinsman, I realized that my own personal connection to the natural world was considerably delayed by my Southwestern boyhood. Where I grew up, everything had thorns or stingers or fangs; you never turned over a rock without dodging possible scorpions or centipedes, you kept a worried eye out for rattlesnakes. You did not brush aside a frond of green without checking it carefully first: even the plant life could do you mayhem. It took decades for me to learn to trust anything out-of-doors. Sometimes, as in northern New Hampshire in February, I think I shouldn't have learned that yet. But it was beautiful up there.

· ·

Tonight is the broadcast date of Willy's *Nova,* made in conjunction with *The Gulf Stream.* He's in Washington, promoting the book. We leave day after tomorrow on vacation, and I'm too distracted to do more than run last-minute errands. The loop trail is glare ice, and in honor of not going to the Caribbean with a limb in a cast, I'm sticking to lower ground.

47

*Writers read literary biography, and surround themselves with
other writers, deliberately to enforce in themselves the
ludicrous notion that a reasonable option for occupying
yourself on the planet until your life span plays itself out is
sitting in a small room for the duration, in the company of
pieces of paper.* —Annie Dillard

M A R C H

· · · · · · · · · · · · · · · · ·

iscellaneous Caribbean notes: We swam
every day, surrounded by species of fish as
unlike each other as they can be and still
swim in the same ocean, yet each looking perfectly efficient at
what it is. They remind me of a good fighter plane, so all-of-
a-piece that the shape alone tells you it's a sweet flyer. I spent
one long snorkel looking closely at a two-foot trumpetfish
(*Aulostomus maculatus*), a slim, gar-looking thing with fins in
what seem like inappropriate places but that turn out to be
just the right places after all for a fish like that. If you're going
to give a fish a head like that, a snout like that, that kind of
small hump in the back, then this is where the fins have to
go. Fins located in this manner enable the fish to swim backward, to hover, to float vertically as well as horizontally. When
you disturb it, it looks back at you over its shoulder—without
having a shoulder, without being able to turn its head.

··

. . . .

Caribbean pace: watching the sun set, watching boats come over the horizon and approach so slowly, watching waves, sailboats, the speed at which the locals walk. Watching fish drift languidly underneath the surface. Everything moves at a measured pace. A boat passes three hundred yards away, and by the time its wake finally laps at your feet, you've forgotten the source of the waves. At sunset the frigate birds soar slowly overhead—for what must be pleasure, they don't look like they're earning a living. Even the lizards move slowly, except for quick little bursts of escape and capture. The locals must think we're crazy just for the pace at which we walk; the hardest part of the service business for them must be learning to accommodate our frenzy.

But they show a frenzy of their own when they get control of a throttle, automotive or marine. Their motorboats zoom everywhere, and the island is spotted with wrecked cars.

• •

Sitting on our hotel room balcony, watching the sunset—as we do religiously, every day—C. notices a sunspot. Through binoculars it looks like nothing more than a particularly dark little dot of cloud, but it descends with the sun, holding its position against the disk. When we get back among newspapers we will learn of an unusually impressive sunspot, and will see the resulting aurora borealis a couple of nights after we are back in New England.

• •

Back home, I fetch the dogs from the boarding kennel and take them immediately around the loop, in fifty-degree weather. They are crazed with happy freedom, we are bathed in their joy. They're definitely fattened up after their incar-

49

ceration; the cats, who stayed home with a house sitter, are thinner. The man at the kennel says cats miss the house, dogs miss the people.

There's a quarter of an inch of new snow over solid ice on the path; neighbors report mostly rain and cold while we were gone. But the warm winter holds: the local paper says that bluebirds have been seen in town every month of the past year.

· ·

Another glorious, blue-sky, no-wind day, comfortable on the loop in shirtsleeves. I added up the cost of our vacation this morning, and, sobered, cranked out a *Runner's Log* before noon. My plan is to spend this week getting caught up, then plunge next week into the New Hampshire piece. Get research started, collect the maps, start finding out about the geography.

· ·

Cleaned up files this morning, getting notes organized before switching my attention to the New Hampshire piece. Most of my notes are made first on a pocket tape recorder, then transcribed. Climate drove me to this embarrassingly technological solution: pens freeze up, pencil leads break, my penmanship is even more illegible than usual when my hands are cold. The tape recorder has proved highly productive as a working method, once I got over my diffidence about talking into a machine while strolling around in the woods. At first I couldn't get out of my head that beautifully loony scene in *Nashville* with Geraldine Chaplin walking through a junkyard, orating about American excess into her hand-held mike. But I was reading the autobiography of William Butler Yeats at the time, and found in that a workable antidote. Unable to take my own thoughts seriously enough to record them, I asked myself what he would have done. Yeats, I decided, would have made the notes. Okay, I could too.

Once I was comfortable with the recorder, I expected it to gather up great profundities and sharp-eyed natural observation, but that seldom happens. It is more like a private secretary, helping me keep straight the details of the business side, taking memos about what needs to be acted upon and how. When I do manage to work on a piece of writing, walking encourages me to brainstorm, to throw everything into the pie. When I transcribe my notes, most of that gets thrown away, as I try to get back some kind of control.

Transcribing notes from our vacation, I am struck by the difference between notes dictated in C.'s presence and those done alone. When she can listen, a formalized diction comes into the tape, a phoniness; I sell harder than in the notes I make when alone. I put more expression, more inflection, into my speech. More like Geraldine Chaplin.

It is as difficult for me to dictate notes in her presence as it was for me to start making oral notes in the first place. C. sweetly interprets this as evidence that we're still courting each other; that I'm still concerned, after twenty-five years together, with making a good impression on her. She is correct.

• •

For this particular long magazine article I'm setting up five computer files, labeled NOW (notes about our recent New Hampshire trip and subsequent visits); PERS (personal memories of living in the area); LORE (various New Hampshire legends, jokes, folk history); SCI (the physical geography); and TXT (the piece itself). My software allows me to flip back and forth among these files. I'll type my notes one time, then toss them electronically into the appropriate files.

Those notes will be very rough; the job then will be to expand and develop the ideas in them, to put them into effective sentences, to try to make them fit the flow of the piece. When it comes time to write the text proper, I'll be pulling paragraphs out of the files and dropping them into place. If I get stuck—if I'm having trouble advancing the text or figuring out where to go with it next—I can always go to any of the five files and start sharpening the paragraphs there, before they're tossed into the text. That process usually generates enough new thoughts to get me going again on the piece itself.

The power of this working method—for me—is that it lets me work as if the writing of the piece is just a case of cutting and pasting. It breaks into manageable pieces the otherwise daunting job of putting together a long, organized piece. When I lose headway in one place, I can always find someplace else to put my time until the next step makes itself clear. As a working method it is very self-protective, saving me from ever having to face a blank sheet of paper.

• •

A textbook March day, very fine but with a blustery north wind. C. is off gathering material for a magazine column, following a real-estate salesman around, being a journalist. I'm in one of those spells when the work is going so well that I'm beginning to worry if it can possibly be any good.

• •

The weather gets into these pages because I do the best part of my work outdoors, walking. Details about the weather go into my journal as an aid to rewriting, intended to help put me back, mentally, into the day in question when I look over the manuscript. The weather is also a device to make me pay a little different kind of attention to the days as they go by. This is part of what writing is intended to do, I think. I have this delusion that reciting my experience to myself makes me acquire it more surely.

Every few pages in Updike's memoir he slyly includes a sentence or two that gives the reader some startling personal insight. After paragraphs of sleepy description or narrative, one gets a quick, offhand glimpse of what he's really driving at. As a reader one begins to anticipate these glimmers, to look forward to them: sweets, hidden in the bread.

. .

St. Patrick's Day, forty degrees at dawn. On the way into town I saw a work crew at roadside, leaning on fenders, turning their faces to the sun.

. .

When *NEM* started up in our own backyard, with friends on staff and my wife as managing editor, it seemed a natural place for me to sell a lot of magazine writing, but it didn't work out that way. If I got into an editorial disagreement, C. found her position untenable, so I pretty well stayed out of those pages. I signed up for the New Hampshire piece only for a chance to work with Todd.

My resistance to magazine writing has a lot to do with what has become the standard magazine piece, which I find extremely painful to do. *NEM* avoids them, but most magazines fill their pages with what C. calls the three-paragraphs-and-a-quote story. The editors ask for a story that says X, Y, and Z; the writer's job then is to call ten or fifteen authorities on the subject and get quotes that say X, Y, and Z. If the authorities you call insist on saying A, B, and C, you simply call more authorities. Some surprisingly prestigious magazines still depend on this technique. An editor for *The New York Times Magazine* asked me for just such a piece a few months ago. I said okay if I could develop the subject on my own, but I wasn't going to do one of those stories where you call fifteen people, trying to extort supportive quotes. "Well," this editor said, "would you call *three* people?"

There's a fundamental contradiction in being determined to wrench out a living by writing alone, and being unwilling to do certain not terribly entertaining but adequately remunerative writing jobs. I have no right to complain about money when I choose not to do some of the things that would make money but would be unpleasant—or humiliating—to do.

. .

One morning in 1972, when we were living in New Hampshire, a young local contractor named Tad Glover stopped by to say that he was running for town policeman—at that time an elective office. Tad said he wanted to break up the "geriatric block" in town government. We were a little taken aback, it being unheard of actually to campaign for a town office, but agreed to give him our vote. At the time the town of Easton was of two cultures, the younger considerably more casual than the older in attitudes toward things like covering one's nakedness when swimming in local streams. Not that we were particularly repressed by the town cop we had, but our sympathies were with the young, and a less inhibiting level of law enforcement sounded like a good idea.

Tad gathered considerable support among the town's younger voters, but forgot that the old get up earlier than the

young. That year's town meeting was called to order at eight
a.m., and by eight-fifteen we were voting. A lot of Tad's voters
didn't show up until ten.

The first ballot for the cop's job was split at something like
twenty-one to twenty-one, and there being no provision for
breaking a tie, we voted again, hoping that someone would
change a vote or a straggler would show up. Each ballot required that slips of paper and pencils be handed out, names
written in, slips collected and laboriously unfolded and tallied.
We went through at least four ballots. Finally, a crumpling of
will, a change of a vote, and Tad was our new police chief.
Someone then pointed out that he couldn't take office; the
gun and the badge were locked in Dick Gawel's garage, and
Dick had gone to Florida for the winter. We'd be without a
cop until Memorial Day. The crime rate did not appreciably
rise.

· ·

Today is the vernal equinox—and about fifteen minutes
after the specific moment (10:28 a.m.), C. spotted the first
robin.

· ·

New Hampshire: I'm struck now by how little we actually
used those mountains when we lived there. We lived and
worked in their shadow, but somehow didn't have much time
for them. Perhaps that's the irony of the piece: how we lived
in a "recreational" region, but how little the recreational re-
sources had to do with our lives, how insulated we were from
that. I was writing for *Skiing* at the time, and skiing on some
mountain or other most of the winter, but actually visited our
local ski area, Cannon Mountain, no more than four or five

times during all the years we lived there. There wasn't time (and by then I'd stopped skiing for fun).

The plan is to do the piece with hard paragraphs of geological and geographical material, interspersed with short takes of reminiscence, memoir, nostalgia, personal response. Memories now pop into my head faster than I can get them down. One local dairy farmer and his wife also ran a large sugaring operation in the spring. Dairy farming is legendarily draining work all by itself. Eventually the load got too great —or romance too strong—and the wife ran off with another man. Hated to lose her, her husband said: she was a good worker.

Or, similarly, another local legend (for the LORE file): a few decades back an elderly Easton farmer came down with ailments beyond the scope of local medicine. His wife took him to Boston to consult with specialists. The diagnosis done, the city doctor laid out a complex course of treatment; the wife inquired about the cost, and was given a figure. "Nope," she said, gathering her purse, "he ain't wuth it," and she took him home, and he died.

In our early years there, the government began studying possible new routes for Interstate 93. Environmental concerns had stalled the highway just south of Franconia Notch, and pressure was building to push it on through. One way of increasing the pressure was to propose that it go elsewhere— our valley, for instance. The blueprints showed a cloverleaf that would erase both our house and the Easton town hall. I personally got a little exercised about this, and vowed to fight it. I posted maps showing the proposed new route, attempting to stir public discussion. I wrote broadsides and distributed them, fancying myself something of a latter-day Paul Revere.

At the height of my campaign a local farmer came by the

house to pick up a poster. He was in his seventies, a tiny wisp of a man but with huge, gnarled hands. He had farmed the valley all his life. "What I don't understand is why you're doing this," he said as he stood in our kitchen. "Easton," he said, *"it ain't nethin'."*

Now I remember my suspicion when he said that: that mixed in it was disappointment at lost possibilities, that the highway might raise his land's value, even make him rich. His subsequent behavior—he not only wouldn't develop his land, he wouldn't even fix up his place or paint his barn—indicates that my suspicions were unfounded.

. .

God's joke: on the first day of spring we get the largest snowfall of the year, about six inches.

. .

My working habits are now built entirely around electronic writing, or, as the fatuous current locution has it, word processing. Working on a computer is not for everyone. I certainly resisted it at first, then fell in love with it. Learning to use a computer was appropriately frustrating, but I went through that drudgery on the final draft of a book that had been composed on a typewriter. One thing I learned was that the compression in working time with electronic writing gave a much better overview of the work.

Learning to use the computer means acquiring a new set of personal metaphors; the ones that occurred to me had to do with circuit grids and storage spaces, with electrons zipping to this or that address, with direct lines of access and efficient routings. The technical accuracy or inaccuracy of these images was beside the point: they enabled me to write on the machine.

More important, they somehow seemed to imply that electronic writing might shorten the distance between the idea and the sentence. I had this vision of electrons snapping into place, canceling discontinuities; it made me want to write sentences that don't do anything but fill the last gap necessary to make the idea come clear.

These images, coupled with the ease of revision, made it easier to admit when a sentence was bothering me. Recognizing this meant acknowledging that the sentence wasn't saying what I wanted to say, which meant I didn't know what I wanted to say, didn't know where the thought was headed, was whistling past the graveyard. It was—is—embarrassing. Most of what I thought I'd learned about writing seemed to be tricks for disguising sentences that didn't quite hit their mark.

After a few months, I began to think I could sniff out electronic writing, not only the bad (which is much worse than old-fashioned manual bad writing) but also the good. The bad stuff comes from the sheer physical ease of production, I guess, inviting what one editor I know calls the puke-out. That's the most common, and valid, complaint about writing electronically. What that complaint overlooks is how beautifully succinct and accurate good electronic writing can be if the writer gains control of it.

Of course there are writers for whom electronic writing is crippling rather than enabling, just as there are one-draft writers. Perhaps each of us does his real work at a different point in the process, but I suspect that the same amount of work is required to get it right. Maybe the ones who don't succeed are those who give up too early on getting it right.

Whether or not I'll ever learn to write the spare and bony

sentences that I dream of, working on a computer is second nature now. I no longer think much about it, perhaps unfortunately. That doesn't mean I've stopped relishing its power. The first level of that is the power to organize—as in keeping multiple files handy, and flipping back and forth between them—which saves huge amounts of time over nonelectronic working methods. But the real power of electronic writing—the philosophical, the almost metaphysical power—is the power to *cut*.

· ·

Now we get a beautiful high-pressure day, snow gradually melting, trickling brook noises alongside the trail; woods as beautiful as they get. The surface of the snow is covered with snow fleas. When you look up through the maples, the tracery of branches against the clear blue sky is like the tracery of veins on the retina. Nice metaphor, but what the hell do you do with it, eh? What's more useless than a poetic metaphor you don't have a place for?

· ·

After long thought, C. is submitting her proposal as is, without revision to suit an agent she doesn't agree with. She really wants to work with Todd, and will accept less money to do so. So the proposal goes formally to Houghton Mifflin after all.

Her resistance to revision is philosophical and, I think, correct. The agent wanted her to turn it into a voyage of self-discovery instead of the biographical and historical book that she wants to write. Of course there's going to be plenty of self-discovery in the book, but C. can't bring herself to write a proposal that predicts self-discovery. She's too reserved—and, perhaps, new to the process—to be able to say that about her own work.

• •

Because I have a couple of good ideas working for me— and, no doubt, because there's some money in the bank— right now it seems fairly easy to write books for a living. If you can write, it would seem not too difficult to find some subject that people will be curious about, go off and learn about it, then write a book about what you learned. Being a writer of nonfiction books doesn't seem perishingly difficult; it just requires a certain amount of energy and an intelligent interest in the world. And a certain accumulated skill at organizing the materials that one's research gathers.

This assumes a benevolent and supportive publishing industry. As it happens, the winds blow back and forth through publishing, giving tough times and easy times; at the moment —this month, anyway—the climate is gentle. But the scheme as I describe it involves the writing of midrange books, and that may not be possible for much longer: as Todd puts it, selling a four-hundred-thousand-dollar proposal is almost easier these days than selling a forty-thousand-dollar one. I've been lucky enough to find in the publishing business a kind of patron. It has been willing, most of the time, to keep people like me alive while we do research and learn the craft (and, most astonishingly, indulge our own curiosities). This benevolence is selective.

Critics of the publishing industry say acquisitions and mergers are wiping out the midrange book. Effort spent on a midrange book doesn't produce as much profit as effort spent on a blockbuster. If you have noticed a certain difficulty in finding interesting books to read in the bookstore, this may be the explanation.

At any rate, say business analysts, that's how publishers think. Writers—who watch, stunned, as meretricious trash continues to make its way onto the best-seller lists—understandably think differently. We have trouble disabusing ourselves of the notion that if the time and energy were spent, midrange books would be profitable too, and the business would be healthier. ("Diversity and stability are so closely intertwined as to seem two names for one fact."—Aldo Leopold) Midrange books could be successful, midrange writers could afford to do the work they do best, everyone could come out ahead.

To be a writer is to be a shuttlecock in a badminton game, one racquet of which is naïve optimism and the other a cynical despair.

• •

It's almost hot this morning; I'm in jeans and shirtsleeves —and rubber boots, there being almost six inches of snow still in the woods. I'm out on the loop early, wanting to get a look at this mountainful of vegetative matter all swelled up and waiting to burst into new growth. Last night C. and I were remembering what it's like at this season in New Hampshire, where the northerly location and higher elevation make the growing season so much shorter. Up there, when the new vegetation finally emerges it seems almost to explode.

The local woods are in a suspended state, halfway to budding above the ground, their feet still stuck in six inches of snow. I thought last night, but didn't have the sentimentality to say it, that springtime is C.'s favorite season but not mine:

61

. . . .

too raw for my tastes. At least until she showed me how to see it. It's still not my favorite, but I am enjoying it more with each passing year.

Had to take off my shirt; it's really *hot*.

• •

My dream is to achieve a state in which I no longer need to write for a living, in which the ability to continue doesn't depend so directly on the sheer volume of product. My fantasy is that this would enable me to cut down, weed out, publish only the writing that truly works: writing successful enough to subsidize itself, to subsidize my writing time. Noble enough sentiments, but what's behind it is probably laziness: I'd like to reduce the work load.

• •

There's four feet of open water around the circumference of the pond. The bluebirds are back, a phoebe this morning, robins and tree swallows everywhere.

I guess I'm an armchair outdoorsman. I've always enjoyed the literature of exploration, for example, but not necessarily the act. Now C. and I are talking about a long canoe trip for her book project, the scary step into direct experience, which of course is what Marty is talking about with his machete image. In the end, all writing is about turning experience into words.

I want to explore that transition point, but I'm not sure how to get at it. Writing, I think, is always a kind of debriefing. As hypnosis reveals in eyewitnesses, there's a great deal more experience in our lives than we ever succeed in knowing. Writing is an attempt to acquire more of it. That seems like a worthwhile undertaking: effectively increasing one's time on earth by increasing the content of that time, instead of numbing out and slipping over the top of it.

. .

I've spent the morning trying to make ideas clearer, trying to make sentences pop like a fastball in the catcher's mitt. In early drafts, I'm always surprised to find paragraphs in which I've said the same things four or five different ways. I think I'm advancing the argument, but I'm really just trying several ways of saying the single small idea I have in mind. The process of rewriting is mostly a process of fighting through that thicket of sentences, cutting back to the one that says what's actually meant.

When I'm working this way, I have the feeling I'm falling on the subject like a terrier on a rat—shaking it, twisting it, pummeling it, throwing it up in the air and trying to catch it in new ways. The terrier, I notice, doesn't take time to think the problem through.

I'd prefer to rewrite—I do in my fantasies—as if bolting together a spherical diving bell. Too much torque on one nut will cause it to gap somewhere else; I want to work my way over the surface systematically, pulling a sentence taut here, finding then a little more slack over there, on the other side, to take up. When I'm done, I should be able to dip the product in a tank and find it finally watertight.

. .

C. has been granted a one-month residency at a writers' colony in the Adirondacks for September. This puts her at least symbolically under way on her book, it seems to me, with or without a contract. It's a nice confirmation, getting her started in a businesslike way. Looks like I get to do a lot of canoeing next year.

. .

Willy, meanwhile, is groaning from a double whammy: in addition to the failure of *Publishers Weekly* to review his book, he now discovers that because of a last-minute title change, the book is listed in *Books in Print* under the wrong title—which means that booksellers will have trouble even finding it when a customer wants to order a copy. So two of the precious little threads that might allow a midrange book to stay alive have been snipped.

· ·

Ice storm. Halfway around the loop, in thick fog, I stop for a moment to enjoy the silence, and a limb comes crashing down: a lot of God's own pruning going on, in dead-still, fog-laden, icebound, wet spring woods. Stop to pluck a maple-twig popsicle. The falling limbs make a lot of noise, breaking loose showers of ice crystals. These are bizarrely beautiful woods today, a little war-torn, a little droopy, but gorgeous. If the sun were to come out it would be dazzling. In the fog it's pretty dazzling anyway.

Those sentences are good and well discharged which are like
so many little resiliencies from the spring floor of our life—a
distinct fruit and kernel itself, springing from terra firma.
Let there be as many distinct plants as the soil and the light
can sustain. Take as many bounds in a day as possible.
Sentences uttered with your back to the wall.
                                    —Henry David Thoreau

                                    A P R I L
• • • • • • • • • • • • • • • • • • • •

A two-day ice storm is finally easing, in bright
sun and a raw, noisy north wind. The ice,
melting and falling from the trees, is beautiful in the sun, but comes crashing down at such a rate one
almost doesn't dare look up to see it. Small hailstorms are
coming down all around us. Pawnee (our black Lab) doesn't
seem to mind, but Molly (the golden retriever) is panicky,
walking almost underfoot, looking worriedly up at me with
every other step. I don't blame her—the loop is a wild and
spooky place this morning.

At the high point of the loop the trees are solid ice; a little
lower there's a clearly defined line below which the sodden
boughs are recovering from their recent burden. Struggling
to describe this melt-line to myself, I realize it needs a good
metaphor. Writing about the natural world—or about science,
same thing—is almost always a matter of coming up with the
right metaphors. I ran across a fine one recently in K. C. Cole's

                                    65

Sympathetic Vibrations: "Matter is frozen energy." $E = mc^2$ is great science; matter as frozen energy is great science writing.

• •

Frozen energy is what one ends up with when one takes on the wrong project. Some kinds of writing are more debilitating than others, and it took me years to learn which, for me, is which. Instructional writing—the pure how-to article —is the worst. Back when I regularly committed that particular sin, my fellow automotive journalists and I used to groan to each other about the annual How-to-Winterize-Your-Car piece. Success as a freelance, we agreed, would mean never again having to tell people how to get their cars ready for winter.

There's a large amount of this kind of writing to be done, and it is possible to make a good living doing it, but the writers who do tend to be the tiredest, most depressed people you'll ever meet. More than once in the past I've come up with a writing project that looked profitable but the doing of which promised a level of drudgery that stopped me cold.

One reason those pieces sap one's soul is that they are presented as completely authoritative, when the writer knows in his heart that there is no authority. There's a definition for you: a writer is someone who knows that there is no authority.

• •

A couple of years ago someone sent me a book called *Laughing in the Hills,* by Bill Barich. I was struck by how quickly, within a sentence or two, I knew I was in the hands of a competent writer. I could feel myself relax and start paying attention to what he had to say. The experience reminded me of a magazine assignment that sent me to Carroll Shelby's school for racing drivers. Shelby liked to talk about how a car "took a set" when it entered a turn, about how you had to get the car "balanced up." I wasn't sure what he was talking about until I'd driven fast through a lot of turns.

When a car is diverted from a straight line, its weight shifts. This shift is taken up by the suspension, the mechanism responsible for keeping the tires firmly in contact with the road no matter how bumpy the surface. At racing speeds, until you feel that weight transfer happen, you have no real confidence that you know what the car is going to do: the transition from stable, straight-ahead loading to stable side-loading is an unknown—and spooky—action, still to come. Once the car's weight is committed to the turn, it hunkers down on its suspension, the tires bite as hard as they're going to bite, and you have a dependable universe of sensory input from which to judge how fast you can go.

A good sentence is like that, I think. It gives the reader confidence in the writer's use of the language. It brings you up to the difficult parts securely, so you can let go of your nervous attention to how this particular arrangement of words is going to come out. Then you can flow with the ideas that are contained within it.

· ·

Why how-to writing is so exasperating: C. and I have been reading a book about canoeing, with detailed instructions for getting the canoe to do what it has to do in various kinds of difficult water. As I read these instructions my attention fogs over, mixed up in language. (I am mildly dyslexic anyway, and have my troubles dealing with right and left in daily life, never mind the additional translation required by the printed word.) I'm sure the writer went out and fiddled around in a canoe until he'd figured out—with his musculature—what was needed to get through the tough spots. Then he sat down and analyzed what he was doing, trying to turn physical action into words.

It's a kind of writing that never works for me. I know as I read it that I'm going to have to spend time on the river to get what he's driving at—and by then I won't really need to read about it anymore. I'm sure there are autodidacts who have the burning concentration to acquire physical skills from books, but I'm not one of them. And I don't think it's particularly useful to try to write that stuff. I know damned well the writing of it is not enjoyable, from experience: *The Sports Illustrated Book of Skiing,* my first book. No fun to do at all.

(I nevertheless proposed another ski book, which was turned down. "A lot of us in the office love to ski," the editor told me, "but we decided we'd rather do it than read about it." Terrific, says I—but then why do all these sex manuals sell so many copies?)

I wrote the *Sports Illustrated* book, in 1971, for a flat fee of two thousand dollars. An agent later told me that the first rule was never to write a book for a flat fee. To demonstrate the point, she showed me that I'd lost about thirteen thousand dollars in royalties. Nobody ever said Time, Inc., was stupid.

• •

I now catch myself dreaming that *Stone Work* is going to lever me out of the world of category books. Writing about athletics and athletic physiology, as I've done for the past several years, is in the end depressing because no matter how it's done, it is going to be read by people—athletes, sports enthusiasts, fitness nuts, even scientists—who aren't particularly interested in writing. It is an audience for whom the value comes through information, which is the one thing that

I've grown tired of dispensing, that I've actively come to distrust. After dealing in it for all these years, I find myself wanting to say, "Can't you see, information doesn't work *either*."

Now I am happily and productively at work on another noncategory book, and see lying ahead of me, still vague but beginning to take shape in my imagination, a related body of work that will fill my days for the next five or six years. I am generally euphoric—but how could I not be?

. .

Just watch, I'll show you how. In the shower this morning I realized that with our income tax payment due in ten days, and with property taxes and the next quarterly tax installment coming up by the fifteenth of June, we are essentially broke, or will be by midsummer, despite having ten thousand dollars in the bank. It's some kind of cosmic joke; I spend the first of the week rolling around in joy at how well my "career" is going, my smugness quotient completely off scale, and then I wake up broke.

"If you chase after money and security, your heart will never unclench," says the *Tao*. I've just had three months of working not in pursuit of money and security, and it was a great relief. What hurts now is having to go back to that hysterical little edge: get this out, get this done, get this sold. My plan was to take a day off, write letters, try to enjoy how well things were going; now I discover I can't concentrate on anything but paying bills. Every time I start to think about the next step, even in the New Hampshire piece, it seems somehow too expensive to do.

. .

Walking the loop is considerably more than a visit with a private secretary. I also mull over organizational and structural matters having to do with whatever piece of writing I have going. I think a lot about the order of attack, or of presentation. While I'm walking I spend less time thinking about the subject itself than about how the elements of the piece fit together. I'm not sure any of these thoughts would make sense to someone else; my notes say things like "move the line about raspberries after the place where the dogs smelled the bear." Put A with B, or maybe slip in C between them: I find myself nailing down the transitions.

Transitions do become an obsession. Having discrete thoughts about a subject is not hard. It's not too hard even to write those thoughts into sentences that develop the ideas you're driving at. But to earn the right to do the easy part, you have to take the reader through a natural progression. One thought has to lead coherently into the next. Finding the way to pull together these disparate elements sometimes seems the hardest part of making a piece work.

When you can't find the transition, it is because you want to make a large leap and are not yet sure why. You know it is time to talk about a new thing, but you're not yet sure why this is the time to talk about it, why it fits in here. To write the transition you have to find out why; you don't get the right to make the leap until you get at the reason underneath.

We do have to depend on our universal but unconscious sense of story. A good sentence is a little story. It resolves its own internal tensions; it does this by getting said what you intend to get said with it—even if that sometimes builds more tension. If it doesn't, it doesn't satisfy. If the transitions aren't there, the piece doesn't satisfy. Only when you are satisfied by the sentences, and satisfied by the transitions, are you able successfully to go on.

. .

About a year into the first draft of *Stone Work* I dragged to a halt, confused about how to continue. The first hundred or so pages were simple narrative, describing, approximately as it happened, the process of building a stone wall. By itself this didn't feel sufficient to make a book, but I wasn't particularly worried. I had a vehicle that allowed me to talk about anything I liked, and I had a sizable additional agenda, but I didn't know quite how to get at it.

Reluctantly, I sent this undigested portion of manuscript to my editor, looking for guidance. Her reaction was lukewarm, which did not give me new impetus. Reluctance validated, not to mention considerable gloom: I am always furious with myself for exposing work too early. There is a justifiable limit to the patience of people who read for a living, and too rough a draft inevitably taints subsequent readings, forcing more polished versions to overcome an unnecessary handicap.

I put the manuscript aside for a couple of months, in hopes that time would let me see it fresh. (I'd run out of money again anyway.) When I picked it up again, I realized that the structure that I had been expecting to emerge "organically" wasn't there, but that to plan the damned thing out ahead of time would not actually be cheating: to put up an armature, so to speak, onto which to start slapping all these wads of words.

Before attempting to push the manuscript forward, I wrote an outline with a tight, five-line description of each of fifteen chapters. This armature was revised almost daily, as parts of the writing fell into their proper place, but I never again lost momentum on the book.

Planning of this kind is architectural, spatial, almost preverbal. As I work through a shorter piece, I have a growing sense of the overall structure that finally tells me which part fits where, but I seldom formally analyze structure. Maybe I should learn how.

• •

By a strange coincidence today's *Times* contains the obituary of Harold T. P. Hayes and a letter to the editors from David E. Davis, Jr. I hadn't heard from, or of, either man in years, but both figured heavily in my early writing days. Davis was the editor of *Car and Driver* who hired me for my first job on a national magazine; Hayes was the editor of *Esquire* during one of its glory periods. He published Norman Mailer's political reporting in the 1960s, gave Tom Wolfe his first major exposure, regularly filled his pages with Terry Southern, Gay Talese, and other exemplars of New Journalism. Truman Capote, James Baldwin. A couple of times in the mid-sixties, when I grew dissatisfied with my lot in the writing business, I tried to get a staff job at *Esquire.*

It was Dave Davis who, as the new editor, had plucked me out of technical writing in Denver and brought me to New York. We'd corresponded but hadn't met, and hit it off immediately. As I remember it, the first piece of writing that Dave produced for *Car and Driver,* on that first day in the office, was a caption for a photo of a Ferrari's exhaust system. It described the tailpipe as approximately equal in size, and loveliness, to Audrey Hepburn's throat. He handed me that line, wretchedly typed on a piece of manuscript paper; I read it, hooted with laughter, and saw doors open ahead of me. This magazine did not have to be all axle ratios and zero-to-sixty times. We could try to infuse it *all* with some kind of creative spark, refuse to let a dull line go into type. Why the hell not try to have some fun with it? At that moment, for the first time in my life, working for a living got truly interesting. I was thirty years old.

Davis became my second writing mentor (after my brother Judson, a poet). What he taught me had more to do with freedom, with the possibility of taking risks, than it had to do with the craft itself—or, for that matter, with putting out magazines. We worked well together, materially improving the magazine (and tripling its circulation), and were great friends for about a year. Magazines are all-consuming, however, and so, in those days, was friendship with Dave. After a while there seemed to be no life outside the world of car magazines. My wife at the time, a bred-in-the-bone Texan, was miserable living in Queens, and the kids weren't too happy either. When an ad agency offered a copywriting job in Detroit, I took it. Dave saw my defection as a betrayal—which I suppose it was, but of him, not of me and mine.

. .

Writing advertising was more like retirement than work, but the move to Detroit did not reverse a rapidly deteriorating domestic life, and the marriage crashed. Within a year I was looking around for another magazine job. On a hunch I wrote a smart-aleck letter to Harold Hayes, explaining why he needed me at *Esquire*. Astonishingly, he responded, asking for some story ideas as indication of my grasp of *Esquire*'s view of the world. I sent a few, which he seemed to like well enough. If ever a staff position opened up, he said, I would be considered for it, but I should understand that I would be entering at a very junior level.

Meanwhile Bill Ziff had acquired *Skiing*, and asked if I wanted to come work on it. I jumped at the chance. The sport of skiing was fine but the job turned out to be hideous; after several months of hard labor on a not very interesting magazine, I started looking for an escape. I turned again to Hayes, sending him a harsh review of the current *Esquire,* criticizing everything from writing styles to cover blurbs.

He invited me in for an interview. I remember him as tall, courtly, a very serious Southerner. What he needed, he said, was someone to save October. It was late spring, and the October issue should have been planned and in the works. October was back-to-college time, the biggest issue of the year, and it needed some blockbuster theme over which to drape brilliant magazine pieces. None of this had been adequately done.

Saving October was only a metaphor, of course—he needed someone to save November and December and all the rest—but if I wanted a job I should figure out how to save October. You betcha, I said, heading for my typewriter, but when I got there I froze. Every big theme I could think of was a weak derivative of some past issue of some other magazine, and none of them had been all that great in the first place. I spent a couple of days wrestling with the problem, but continued to draw blanks. Before long I began to feel, petulantly, that the problem was not with me but with the concept, that saving October was the wrong way to think about magazines. I'd never liked big-theme issues anyway. If as a reader you aren't interested in the single theme to which the issue is tied, then the whole thing is a waste. And other rationalizations.

Hayes had also told me that at the weekly staff meeting every editor had to produce five new story ideas. I wrote him an impassioned explanation of why I'd decided not to save October, and attached a single typewritten page, single-spaced with narrow margins, completely filled with story ideas: a hundred and thirty-five stories I thought *Esquire* should do. No thanks, said Hayes. He'd proposed a problem and asked me to demonstrate my ability to solve it; instead of a solution, he got an argument about magazine philosophy. I said we should let good writers write about what stimulated them most, and what would save October would grow out of that. He replied, "I would rather rely on any five neurotic, crippled, illiterate editors than on the fifteen best writers in town."

Looking back at that correspondence, I can't help wonder how my life would have changed if I'd saved October. I'd probably have spent a lot more years involved in that kind of serious magazine effort. But I failed, and continued in the magazine business for only one more year. That year made it much easier to quit—to give up the crazed level of effort that magazines require—than it might otherwise have been.

• •

My panic attack in the shower was really only at having to turn my head back to making money. I thought I was going to have time to work on longer, less commercial projects, but I'm going to have to get back out and hustle. Almost as if I had a real job. That wasn't part of the deal, was it?

Of course C. is hustling away all the time anyway, putting groceries and a lot more on the table. When does she get writing time?

• •

I resigned as editor of *Skiing* but continued freelancing for the magazine for several years. This involved a lot of exotic travel, exotic entertainment, meetings with exotic people. Skiing offered a peculiar jet-set connection with the natural world, but only in that it put you on all those gorgeous mountains. The sport itself, as it was coming to be practiced, put a kind of plasticized distance between the skier and that natural world. Its base—the sport as well as the magazine—was, and is, not nature or the mountains or healthy outdoor activity, but the fashion industry, an irredeemably sleazy economic foundation. In fact it is the fashion industry that eventually takes over most participation sports—and every single one of the successful special-interest magazines.

Not that any magazine maintains its virginity. One of the things I teased Hayes about was a full-color spread in *Esquire* showing a couple of hundred bottles of different brands of men's perfume. He thought that was a pretty slick way of getting all those advertisers off his back at once—and, in all its cynicism, I had to admit that that was what it was: slick.

The unfortunate truth is that the commercial engine militates heavily against good magazines now. New magazines are being started at the rate of something like five hundred a year, but the ones that even aim at being good—literate, intelligent, thoughtful—make up less than one percent of that figure. And the number of those with any hope of surviving financially is very close to zero. The start-up of a good magazine is in many ways the slow and painful process of teaching an idealistic staff how impossible it is to survive as a good magazine. How in the end the commercial engine is going to win, how your integrity is slowly going to be sapped. You're going to give in on this, and then on this, and then that, and then you're going to put a girl in a swimsuit on the cover, and it will sell more copies than any other issue you've done, and you've lost the battle. As a serious magazine, you are dead.

• •

Out of the blue comes a call from Billy Sims of Whittle Communications' *Special Report,* asking for a twelve-hundred-

worder on "listening to the body." I said that if he'd take a
personal essay based on past experience, rather than a piece
of reporting, I'd be delighted. I took the job knowing I'd also
cut the piece in half and get a *Running Log* essay out of it too.
So, a nice little piece of financial rescue comes in over the
transom.

I was talking later with Hans, a fellow freelancer, about
finances. Debt, we agreed—or, in my current case, imminent
debt—is like a deerfly buzzing around your head while you're
trying to prune the roses.

. .

Letter this morning from a man who had discovered an
act of plagiarism from *Truck,* and thus a considerable mystery
is solved. Several months ago the mail brought a mysterious,
abject confession: some poor jerk said he'd lifted an anecdote
from my book, passed it off as his own, and gotten it published
in a small magazine. Someone had caught him and called him
on it, putting him into a blind panic. He was apologizing to
the magazine, to the magazine's readers, to me, to everyone
he could think of. He said he'd only committed two really
dishonest acts in his life: adultery in his first marriage, and
this plagiarism.

The poor fellow was so distraught that I told him to relax,
forget the whole thing, go forth and sin no more. But now I
finally get a clipping of the piece, and when I see what a bald-
faced job he'd done of it, I wish I hadn't let him off the hook
so easily. My original reaction to the plagiarism was correct,
I think—to note it and go on, not tying up memory banks (or
writing time) on the whole silly affair. But plagiarism is theft
of someone's hard work, and does need airing. It happened
to me once before that I know of, a published magazine piece
reprinted in a distant small newspaper under someone else's

name. But that one was just a dumb exercise piece for skiers, and its theft was more amusing than irritating.

• •

Writing time, writing all the time: Lynne Bertrand has just quit her newspaper staff job and gone freelance, and tells me that she finds herself working on her own stuff—quietly, in her head—when she's supposed to be socializing or attending to domestic life. Now she asks, *can we get away with this?* It immediately became a kind of giggling little secret between us: that when you're a writer you get to work on your own stuff all the time.

• •

Hans is reading *Stone Work* in galleys, and teases me about my thickets of parentheses and dashes. His high-school English teacher told him not to write that way. I do have a distressingly ornate set of writing habits. I'm trying to work my way out of them, I swear I am. I really do want to write simple declarative sentences, subject-verb-object, active voice, no punctuation but periods, no words over five or six letters. Maybe a comma every five or six sentences, if I can't write my way around it. A minimum of syllables. (And no more sentence fragments.) I do want to write with that simplicity of style, of expression, that clarity of thought.

But I can't break the old habits. Every time I turn in a manuscript, I suggest that the editors push me in that direction, but when they do they seem invariably to strip the wit and balance out of the sentences, and I can't stand not to put it back in. I do not yet have sufficient control—after thirty years—of my craft.

• •

The morning's mail brings wonderful news: the Book-of-the-Month Club wants *Stone Work* as an alternate selection. It doesn't pay much—and my half goes against the advance anyway—but the attention is very much worthwhile. It also means that more copies will be in print, giving the book a little better shot at surviving. This is the first blip on the screen out there, the first flicker of interest in the book.

. .

Clear skies at dawn, with a heavy sense of burgeoning spring; by the smell I'd judge that local farmers are dressing their fields.

Boston *Globe* columnist M. R. Montgomery recently did a nice little piece on the emergence of woodchucks at this time of year. The woodchucks quickly find that there's nothing green to eat yet and go back down their burrows, but in their brief early-spring reconnaissance, wandering around the fields and meadows, they lay down a whole new world of smells, revivifying the universe for all the neighborhood dogs.

Clouds roll in, and at noon I walk the loop in a gentle, drizzly spring rain, still basking in the news about the book club.

. .

Was able to pay taxes without borrowing. Will be able to do so again on June fifteenth, if we don't eat between now and then.

The only way out of our continuing financial crunch is to get another book contract working soon. My recent book advances have been paid one third on signing, one third on evidence of "satisfactory progress," one third on completion of an acceptable manuscript. As Georges points out, this means that the writer has to be able to complete the book for two thirds of the contract's face amount; the last third becomes a little bonus for completion of the work.

One horrifying rule of thumb of the freelance life is that one must make twice what a wage-earner makes in order to pay one's own "benefits." On that scale, we're living on the equivalent of less than twenty-five thousand dollars per year. We live better than that because we opt not to pay ourselves some of the benefits; we live worse than that from the standpoint of our shaky security. But we have fresh mushrooms for the salad, and I drink the next-most-expensive gin, and we have a bottle of champagne when we have something to celebrate, so I guess we're not hurting too bad. Never poor, always broke.

I no longer own a suit that fits (I bought the last one in 1978, so let's not even talk about style), and C. has no shoes to go to the city in, but that's as much a matter of taste as need or want. Except for the occasional wedding or funeral, we have no need of city clothes. "My main reason for adopting literature as a profession," said George Bernard Shaw, "was that, as the author is never seen by his clients, he need not dress respectably."

One of The New York Times's sillier featurettes recently polled people who work at home about what they wear while they work. I wrote a letter to the editors claiming to be nude at the time except for a whirlie-beanie and skin diver's flippers, but they didn't print it. I wear jeans and a T-shirt ninety-nine percent of my waking hours. Perhaps the energy that would otherwise be devoted to grooming is now applied to sentences. I prefer not to let a sentence go out of the house until I've stood it in front of a mirror, adjusted its tie, slicked down its hair, and polished its shoes.

• •

The next step for me in learning to write better is surely to read my manuscripts aloud. I can't bring myself to do it, partly out of the same diffidence that made it so hard to get started making notes on tape, and partly out of a prejudice from writing speeches, from discovering how simply things must be said to be spoken aloud. This simplification strips the language of so much structural possibility that I unthinkingly consider it a kind of dumbing-down of discourse.

My attempts at public speaking have been disastrous, in part because I insist on writing the speeches and reading them. I don't trust the sentences that will come flowing out of my mouth unexamined. This is simply a lack of confidence. The horrible truth is that all conversation is made up of bad sentences, and, aurally, we understand bad sentences perhaps better than we do good ones. We listen better than we read, and have learned how to edit the bad sentence and get the sense out of it.

· ·

A perfectly fine spring day, mallards on the pond this morning, a little skin of ice around one corner but sixty degrees by noon. C. spent an hour outside listening to birdsong before going off to a lunch date. Not a hint of green except the hemlocks, but the April sun is powerful, and the woods don't feel like November anymore. Too bright in here. It's coming, it's coming.

· ·

Willy and Liz gave me a copy of Brenda Ueland's *If You Want to Write* (Graywolf Press, St. Paul). First published in 1938, it's still a refreshing voice, cantankerous and challenging. (The publisher suggests the book be shelved under "Writing/Psychology"! There's a category I never knew ex-

81

isted.) Ueland is most interesting on how your writing will go bad on you if you aren't absolutely honest in confronting your material. This is a subject that keeps coming up in my own ruminations. I distinctly remember telling a friend, several years ago, that I thought I'd just about gotten all of the dishonesty out of *Truck*—in which I had to fiddle the facts to make two years' experiences fit into one (just as Thoreau did in *Walden*, he said smugly). In the books I've written since, I've worked harder at finding out for myself what is honest and what isn't.

What I think I'm coming to understand is that when a sentence bothers me, it's usually because I'm trying to pull some little con, some swindle, expressing some observation or emotion that isn't truly my own. I'm trying to exaggerate or elaborate the facts more than they will bear. Trying to Be Literary, which distracts me from the hard work of figuring out what I think.

Similarly, the argument for tight writing: it's the only kind of writing that's honest. Writing is only loose because the writer is trying to slip something by you—or doesn't yet know what he's trying to say.

• •

New Hampshire: I want to pin it down with facts but there are no facts, there's just that mountain range, that physical structure looming over one side of the valley. No fact greater than that. How to write about it?

• •

In the sagging middle of the period when I was writing *Stone Work*, I bitched about money to my editor. Maybe, she suggested, I'd have to stop and do some journalism. Take in a little laundry. "We all have to take in washing from time to time," she said. She was right, of course, but her advice sent me into a tantrum that took weeks to get over. I may not be over it yet.

· ·

Gray, sixty degrees, an absolutely undistinguished and undistinguishable day. How does one find something to distinguish it by? I stop to admire a pinecone, its paint job, the swirling Fibonacci sequence that arranges the scales for maximum exposure to the light. I'm staring at it as hard as I can, as if to eat it, attempting to plunder it for a description. As if to memorize it well enough to draw it later.

In *An American Childhood,* Annie Dillard talks about learning to draw as a kid, and about paying attention: ". . . things themselves possessed no fixed and intrinsic amount of interest; instead things were interesting as long as you had attention to give them. How long does it take to draw a baseball mitt? As much time as you care to give it. Not an infinite amount of time, but more time than you first imagined. For many days, so long as you want to keep drawing that mitt, and studying that mitt, there will always be a new and finer layer of distinctions to draw out and lay in. Your attention discovers—seems thereby to produce—an array of interesting features in any object. . . ."

I seldom notice bird calls; if something is going to get my attention I have to see it. When I began to need glasses I hated them for a long time, but I've come to love them. Now I sometimes wish I had the equivalent of eyeglasses to strap onto my other senses, to return them to youthful acuity.

When stymied at work, my instinct is always to go back to the light, to seek the light: find the light, chase the light, describe the light. If I were a dog my attention would surely turn to the air, the stuff that carries the smells. Is it the light that causes me to be dominated by the sense of sight, or is it my domination by the sense of sight that causes me to chase after the light?

· ·

C. dropped by the *NEM* offices, and came home with the remarkable (to me) news that Todd is in France for two weeks—without getting her an answer on her book proposal. She isn't angry about this. Twice I raised the question of her obvious rage; no, she said with a smile, she's given up anger. I'm dumbfounded.

· ·

It is my good fortune, I think, to spend most of my waking time at play with the language. When I'm not reading, I'm writing (or talking). Or gibbering at myself internally, trying out sentences.

It's all just an attempt to come up with the best possible story. The first line of every piece of writing should be, "Let's see, now, what's the best way to tell this?" The writer ought to start with that line in his head. It should never make its way onto the page, of course (except perhaps as a joke, as at the beginning of this book), but it should inform the writer's angle of attack.

C. was telling me about some bit of cat behavior the other night, and exaggerating it sharply, for purely humorous purposes. She put a little spin on it, making the behavior more dramatic—more clear—than it actually was. This, I think, is what storytelling usually is: you take some half-baked experience that went on at the corner of your eye, the full import of which you didn't get because you weren't paying it sufficient attention. Then you recast it in your mind.

I always debrief myself after a trip: I come back and talk about it with C., and thereby find out what happened. I put the experience into a story, a narration, and only then realize how the parts actually fit together. I think I understand what happened more clearly after I've told it.

Perhaps all storytelling, all our myths, come this way. An act or event is observed, and then the observation is developed—exaggerated—into a story. All writers exaggerate. We can't resist the impulse to make the story better than it is, to make our lives richer than they are.

"Show 'em, don't tell 'em," said that scrawled note on my first rejection slip. And I did, I tried to pull the readers inside the experience, to let it happen to them instead of describing it to them. And then the story sold.

But I wonder if the effort to enhance the story—the emphasis and exaggeration that we put onto stories in the process of telling them, if only to ourselves—isn't the very thing that makes us feel inauthentic, that gives us this whispered message that we're living with lies. We know that we lie ourselves, we exaggerate and manipulate, and we know we are being lied to, in all stories, all the time, no matter how we suspend our disbelief.

There is a cute, entertaining, maybe even moving story to be told about the Easton Valley, which would imply that we understood what was going on while we were there, which would be a lie. We select from our experience to tell our stories, and the process of selection is ego-driven: trying to explain, to demonstrate, that we are superior by virtue of the intelligence of our selection.

Well, I defy any writer to get down the sharp comfort, the

soothing invigoration of today's air. Combined with today's sun. How can I take you out with me to feel this air?

• •

New Hampshire piece: lead with the joke we pulled on Hans and Lynne, on the drive in; quickly describe the mountain range; then explain that that valley is where we lived for twelve years, tucked up on the shoulder of Kinsman. That's where C. and I lived from, essentially, young adulthood to young middle age. All our changes, as we used to say, were there. It was ten years ago, and now we're going back to stay in the very same house, on the very same mountainside.

Then I want to drop in a little of the geology/natural history, placing this mountain range in space and time and telling what it amounts to. My geology notes say it was seabed once (wasn't everything?), filled with sediments that ran off another mountain range to the east of where Maine is now. The seabed sedimented and metamorphosed and all that other geologic stuff; turned duff and organic waste and runoff and silt and slop and drainage somehow into rock, got shoved up and worn down and shoved up again, ballooned upward from the pressure of magma boiling in the cauldron below. Laid down twenty thousand feet of sediments and raised that up and eroded it all away, and finally thrust up a fair-sized mountain range. And then some mouse crawled into the gear-teeth of the climate, and all was covered with ice to thousands of feet of additional altitude, which scraped the tops off the mountains and rounded them smooth.

God, the climate. Getting to town on winter mornings could turn into an athletic event. It's not that we lived in fear of the place—we relished it and enjoyed it and didn't let it keep us from doing whatever we wanted to do—but lodged in the back of our minds, in winter anyway, was the knowledge that at any time you could slide off a back road somewhere and disappear, not to be found until spring. It put an unaccustomed judiciousness into our movements.

On the other hand, I remember a visit from a ski-business friend in June, just after a cool front had swept the skies clean. By sunset we would face one of our not altogether rare June frosts, but at midday the world seemed composed entirely of birdsong, bee-hum, and golden light. Every physical object had a sharp outline around it, as if you were looking through high-resolution binoculars. It was one of those times when to sit on the porch and breathe the air was about as much entertainment as one could bear. Our friend had been in the area perhaps fifteen times before, but always in ski season, and he had never quite figured out what the charm was. "*Now,*" he said, taking a deep breath of vanilla-sweet balsam, staring transfixed at the serene stillness of Mount Kinsman, "I understand why you live here."

. .

Last evening I was looking through binoculars across the field below the house, and was shocked at the ripple and swoop in what I'd always regarded as a flat space. It made me think about the good-sized lawn that I mow all summer, and how well I know that terrain at the micro level, every flare and hollow, every flat and angle and hummock.

The idea for the New Hampshire piece came from a visit we made a couple of years ago. We'd gone back up to celebrate a wedding anniversary, staying in a local inn and hiking the familiar hills. After dinner we drove out the Easton Valley, parked near our old house, and strolled around a loop of road that we'd walked almost daily during the years we lived there.

It was a sultry September night, with a full moon, and something about that stroll was very moving. Now I think it was just this, the recognition of the contours, their familiarity, the three-dimensionality of the road surface itself, the dips and hollows and high spots, knowing ahead of time where the pavement would be wet from that spring I've seen seep for twenty years now. That familiarity with the terrain, down there among the ripples of the surface of the land, is the emotional connection I have with the piece of real estate that is the Easton Valley. How to write about this?

· ·

The other day some small idea popped into my head, and I had the strange experience of "watching"—being conscious of it—as it began to form. I observed myself trial-fitting it into a sentence, moving elements around in order to grasp it more clearly. I no longer remember when it happened or what the subject was, but the process itself was clear. I was shocked that it began in such preverbal form.

I tried to describe this to Willy at lunch. He said his father, Archibald MacLeish, told him that he usually got a rhythm in his head first, then found the words that made that rhythm into a poem. That reminded me of a touching story about Yeats: his son remembers the old man, in his nineties, sitting on a porch in the sun in Italy, pounding his hand on the arm of his rocking chair and gradually working out the words to fit the rhythm.

· ·

A rough lead is now carpentered into place in the New Hampshire piece, and I want to stop and describe the mountain range. Maybe I should just self-consciously say, in the text, that the idea was to do a piece about that entire ridge and valley and what it's like to live there. That, however, turned out to be something of a paper premise: when we went back and spent time there, and realized how Mount Kinsman dominated the valley, we found all our attention turned to the single mountain.

There's a mountain at the south end of the valley called Moosilauke that always seemed to be the private stomping ground of the Dartmouth boys—they ski-raced on it for years, built a now-dismantled shelter on top, had a lodge halfway up the side. At the northern end of the valley, all is dominated in mood and aspect by Mount Lafayette, nearly a mile high, a brooding, chilling presence, a mountain obviously struggling with the elements. A series of ravines on the side of Lafayette arrange themselves so that early snows put down the form of a white cross; locals say that the third time you see the cross in the fall—the third coating of snow—it will stay there all winter long.

On the other side of the range is the Notch: the towns of Lincoln and Woodstock, trained bears and moccasin stores, ski shops, amusement parks, kiddie zoos, soft-ice-cream parlors. On the far side of the Notch is Franconia Ridge, a spectacular line of above-timberline peaks, one of the favorite hiking and camping areas in New England. On the far side of that ridge is the great Pemigewasset Wilderness.

Too much material, too wide a lens, for a comprehensible magazine story. Cut like crazy.

• •

Struggling, struggling, with the New Hampshire piece. After months of loose and easy note-taking, there's a shock in trying to do the detail work. I've gotten out of the habit of getting each sentence right before going on to the next.

It's an old working habit that I can't seem to break. I should

89

be picking paragraphs out of the notes that are easily ex-
pandable, that tell good stories or that remind me of areas I
need to cover. I should just be writing those, getting them
done well so I can insert them in the text later. Keep the form
loose, then tighten up, sharpen the transitions, cut and cut
and cut. Instead I'm engraving the Lord's Prayer on the head
of a pin: trying to finish the piece (that's "finish" in the furniture sense) in the first draft.

As an experiment, I'm also talking myself through it, saying
in the text that this is what I'm going to do now, and this is
what comes next, and so on: very self-consciously laying out
how the piece is constructed, as a guidepost for no one but
me. I want to see if this method gives me a better understanding of structure. Once it's written I'll go back and take out all
the extraneous commentary, the self-consciousness.

• •

Outside magazine called yesterday to say they wanted an
excerpt from *Stone Work*—a fifteen-hundred-dollar miracle,
as far as I'm concerned. If they publish it in their July issue,
as planned, the whole sum comes to me. (After publication,
it's split fifty-fifty with the publisher.) It's also wonderful promotion, a large advertisement for the book. Of course I choose
to interpret it as an additional indication of outside interest,
a sign that the book might amount to something. The news
set me afloat for the evening, thinking big thoughts.

It reminds me of the call from my agent, years ago, telling
me that Bantam had put in a substantial floor bid for the
paperback rights to *Truck*. I immediately went outdoors and
began walking around the place in a daze, faking yard work.
After a while I realized a refrain was running over and over
in my head: "big cigars and motorcars" is what it said.

• •

The other night C. was stuck on her next column, so I asked her to talk me through it, tell me what she'd done and how she'd organized it. As she did, I suggested some small thing—I no longer remember what, it doesn't matter—that clicked open another door and got her going again. The very next night she talked me through my day's work in exactly the same way. Sometimes it almost seems an unfair advantage to have two working writers in the house. We understand each other's work sufficiently that it almost doubles the brain power available for any given project. Of course we both then have to go off and do the work, but we have this extraordinarily productive nightly debriefing to keep up steam for the next day.

The ideas that result don't always solve the problem, but they seem to at the time, and give us hope. So we try them, and if they work out, fine, and if they don't we haven't lost anything. In fact we've further triangulated the problem. Found out what works—or why it doesn't. This is good science.

• •

An absolutely soft spring day, after a night of badly needed rain; an Irish day, wonderfully damp, a level of moisture that over the winter has been sorely missed. It's as if everything has been enclosed in a hard shell that needed moistening and softening: now things are popping, buds on everything, greening up. Until we get some green to modify the strong April sun, though, the light is a kick in the face, almost too bright to bear.

• •

The discovery of air: maybe that's the small idea I've been searching for. Water was not discovered by a fish. When you drive into the Easton Valley by the back way, the view suddenly opens up, the horizon jumps back a couple of miles into the distance. There's all this *space* between you and it. Having that wall of mountains, something large and solid out there a huge distance away, makes you aware of the space you live in. You become aware of the atmosphere; you discover the air.

Maybe that's the way of talking about mountains that I've been looking for. They simply make you aware of the space around you. C. points out that the same thing is true of the interior of cathedrals (and barns). Opening up the space you live in makes you realize that you're surrounded by this atmosphere all the time, this benign stuff you breathe, the single most important thing for sustaining life. Maybe when you get a great vista, the lift you get is from the reaffirmation of how much space there is, how much atmosphere.

One thing the piece has to emphasize is that we do have real mountains in New England, and people live there, and their lives are very different from the lives of flatlanders. Their attitudes (and crazinesses) are different, too. I want the piece to be a paean to the good parts of mountain life; I want it to speak of the positive gains of living in that environment. But it must also say that living there is impossible, the cost is too high. It takes a peculiar relish for the vividness of life to keep one there. If you don't have a great appetite for vividness you won't make it in the mountains. We did for a while, but that wore out; then we sought surcease, soul's ease. These foothills of the Berkshires seem, by contrast, almost Floridian.

. . . there are hours and hours of a writer's time that aren't worth the paper he is not writing anything on.
— E. B. White

• • • • • • • • • • • • • • • • • • •

*M*ay begins muggy and gray; blackflies will be swarming any time now, and I'll be mowing by the end of the week.

C. ran into Todd this morning: Houghton Mifflin is not going to make an offer on her book. He's sorry, wishes he had more clout with the company, etc. Says she shouldn't get discouraged, should send it to Knopf, also Farrar, Straus. This is a blow mostly because she won't get to work with Todd, but also a little deflating. I think Todd's right, the book will sell, she'll do it with somebody.

She also found out that the sale of *NEM* is bogged in legal wrangling, so they still don't have money to pay writers. That saps some of the urgency out of working on the New Hampshire piece. I've nevertheless begun calling around among academics, looking for scientific background. None that I reached was particularly helpful, but I did get a lead on a better source, in Vermont, with whom I have an appointment in two days.

• •

Do I have room to tell the story of Sam Ely? He was an Easton legend, a gloomy little gnome of a man, a little "touched" (wonderful expression). He was rumored once to have trained Lippizaner stallions in Austria, and had been a teamster over in the Pemi Wilderness during the timber boom there, under Sherman Adams—who was a lumberman before he went to Washington and got in trouble over vicuña coats, before he came back home and built a ski resort. Local gossip had it that Adams looked out for Sam. Someone needed to: we used to run into him occasionally in the supermarket parking lot, standing on the running board of his truck, shouting curses at the sky.

When we knew him, Sam lived in a little roadside hut built out of scrap lumber and sheet tin, including some old filling station signs that spelled out the word SHESHELLELLELL on its side. He had lived in a succession of houses up and down the valley, almost all of which eventually burned down, perhaps because he found fire a useful tool. The barn next to his shack also burned down: he couldn't get his truck started one cold winter night, built a fire under it to warm the crankcase, and things got out of hand.

Other Easton and Franconia buildings went up in flames from time to time. Sam was always darkly suspicioned, but nothing was ever proved. When he died, we were astonished to learn that he was a Muslim.

• •

I'm struggling to get back into a steady daily working rhythm. "Freelance" conjures up a guy in a trench coat whipping back and forth across the ocean, interviewing political figures and ducking behind enemy lines, which is all very romantic but not terribly productive. My approach to the free-lance life is the opposite: I do everything I can to regularize it, surround it with methodical habits, move it in the direction of a normal job.

I dream occasionally about holding a regular job again, doing the same work every day, knowing where I have to be and what I have to do. My fear of boredom is almost pathological, but the boredom I fear doesn't come from regularity and normalization, it comes from trying to write things that offer no gear teeth for my interest. The most difficult work I know is to write about subjects one is not interested in. You have to do the writing that you *can* do, an axiom I keep repeating to uncomprehending editors.

Even the apparent freedom of a regular weekly or monthly column eventually fades, crippled by the built-in strictures of the publication for which it is written. When my columns began to run dry, I always ended up turning out "service" pieces—how-to, self-help, lists of useful information—based on embarrassingly slipshod research. Which left me dying inside, feeling that I was telling lies.

The unfortunate truth is that at magazine rates of pay, the little research the writer can afford to do is almost guaranteed to be superficial. As a freelance I know the research is always insufficient—but I'm also always afraid I'm spinning off time in pointless searches (usually for quotable "authorities"), afraid the peculiar demands of the publication will somehow nullify what little research I manage to do. I'm afraid the magazine will require endless rewrites to fit a mold that doesn't connect in my mind: an editor's vision that he or she can't quite articulate, or that I don't quite get. That's worse than outright rejection, which at least brings a small kill fee and a chance to sell the piece elsewhere.

But among all the niggling little fears at work in a writer's mind, the worst is of sitting down at the machine and being unable to write. As a writer I've never (knock on wood) blocked. There have been months when I was floundering, never confident that I knew where a project was going and how it was going to work out, but I continued to write, continued to believe I was producing acceptable material. I just didn't know where it was headed.

I've never even known a seriously blocked writer. I've seen writers go through blocked weeks, unable to start something and therefore threatened by increasingly impossible deadlines, but I've never known anyone who's gone through the classical blockage. I suspect it is a fear that lies at the back of every writer's mind, like cancer.

· ·

A steady rain, falling through fog, makes the woods particularly beautiful. It is badly needed, turning everything green, green. Better sharpen the mower blades. Last night C. heard the first hermit thrush of the season. As of yesterday there were five eggs in the bluebird house—and no sixth today, so the fifth egg gives a counting date by which to calculate the hatch.

· ·

The NEM deal is signed, they're paying bills again, and I'm back on the New Hampshire piece. Galleys from Outside's excerpt of Stone Work await me on my desk, and Sims should be calling back for a revise on the piece for Whittle. Driving me nuts. Distractions keep littering the path.

An amusing call from an editor at Whittle: I sent them a rough manuscript, not having a sense of their editorial slant, with a note asking for guidance. The editor who called said that he agrees the piece needs work, but "we can't figure out what it lacks." I am, frankly, going to wait for them to figure that out and tell me. I don't have a clear enough view of what they're looking for to pour time into solving it myself.

Thus the vicissitudes of taking in laundry. When my editor suggested I might have to do that, I decided, in a fury, to go into debt instead, subsidizing myself. I have since sworn never to do that again, but also to seek only projects that would not require me to stop in midcourse to pay bills. Great plan, if it only worked.

Virginia Woolf pointed out the writer's need of a room of her own. I'm not sure she mentioned time.

. .

Yesterday I drove to northern Vermont to interview a free-lance ecologist whom I'll call Dr. Jones, since he doesn't want any personal recognition (a remarkable stance for a freelance anything). To drive that far north brings a discouraging re-entry into winter, but an effective demonstration of one of the points I'll be making about New Hampshire: as Jones put it, in the mountains the seasons are tilted; they're steeper. In the Easton Valley, in my memory, they were damned near vertical.

Jones is a real find, a shy young Ph.D, minding his toddler while we talked, in a study in which baby toys spilled over research materials. He laid out the significance of north country physical geography with great clarity, and pointed me toward half a dozen additional sources. One of them is an archaeologist who has studied cluster farms in mountain valleys of New England. Many of New England's high mountain valleys were settled surprisingly early, in "hill farm clustered communities"—usually eight to ten farmsteads around a road, sharing agricultural information and cooperative labor as well as schools and churches. The cluster that would become Easton was first settled in 1782. He's sending me a monograph.

• •

Great news this morning, a good review for *Stone Work* in *Kirkus*. That newsletter has a reputation for bitchiness, and a favorable review there is jokingly regarded as the kiss of death, but I'll take it. Says it's a "sturdy book."

I keep making the mistake of imagining success. I dream of being able to say, at the end of that book's little life, see, I can write good books, if I can only get the time to do it.

• •

Easton Valley and L'il Abner's dark side: I wonder if the piece should acknowledge that public perception. The popular myth is that isolated mountain villages are populated by hunchbacks and harelips. Tobacco Road. There's a certain basis for this view: some parts of New England mark the northern end of Appalachia. One of our former neighbors was a visiting nurse who knew families back in those woods whose kids missed school for lack of shoes. But that dark side is only a small part of mountain life.

The major town in the valley is Franconia, and there are legends living there, legendary people—great ski racers, for instance, who settled down and now farm, or plow snow and pump gas for a living. There are no legendary people in Easton. (C. once proofread a book about China with the wonderful title *1587, A Year of No Significance*. Maybe I should call the piece "Easton, A Town of No Significance.")

But it isn't known as the Franconia Valley, it's the Easton Valley. Franconia sits at the mouth of the valley, where the Ham Branch empties into the Gale River. The Gale goes on

to form its own pleasant valley as it runs on down to the
Ammonoosuc, but the valley of the Gale doesn't have moun-
tains looming over it. It's just another anonymous valley;
Easton's is the valley that captures the local imagination.
Mountains make the difference.

• •

In the mail this morning came the first copy of *Stone Work*,
the finished book. Looks great, the type a little denser than I
remember from the galleys. The cover art is repeated as section dividers, a nice touch.

One might expect a certain welling up of emotion at the
arrival, after three years of work, of the actual book, the physical object in one's hands: what a writer friend once characterized as a piece of real estate. I must be jaded. It's nice to
have, to know it is manufactured and on its way to the various
places I want it to go, but it's not as big a thrill as perhaps it
should be.

• •

Notes for the LORE file: On the day we moved to Easton,
while we were still hauling furniture, a little old lady came
calling. She did not beat around the bush: did we have any
children? No. Did we plan to have children? No. Well then,
welcome to Easton. Didn't look like we'd be driving up school
taxes.

That was Helen Young, who is no longer with us. She
turned out to be one of the town's most distinguished citizens,
having been, among other things, a state representative long
before women were commonplace in that role. That may be
where she picked up her skill in making pointed inquiries
somehow without giving offense. A first principle of New

Hampshire residence, for example, is that one does with one's place any goddamned thing one wants—as attested to by the tens of thousands of junk cars, rusted-out fifty-five-gallon drums, and defunct push-mowers scattered about people's yards. Helen once had sufficient moxie to violate this principle directly, cornering me after town meeting and sweetly asking when I intended to mow the field next to my barn. I thought I was outraged at the time, but to my surprise I ended up doing it.

• •

The archaeologist sent the wrong papers—no specific references to Easton—but that doesn't matter. With their general discussion, the interview with Jones, and the logging book he put me onto—*Tall Trees, Tough Men,* by Robert E. Pike—I'm getting pretty good triangulation on New England mountain life in previous eras.

Tall Trees is one of those curious pieces of extremely awkward writing that are nevertheless great reads. I had no proper sense of the amount of physical danger in logging. The river drives were exciting events in the lives of northern New England residents. In one drive down the Connecticut, eleven men were lost, out of a crew of five hundred, in the first sixty miles. Despite those statistics, the locals would flock from their farms to sign up for the drives.

They were—are—a people of hard, and hard-won, skills. When we left northern New Hampshire for balmy western Massachusetts, we were shocked at the difference in workmanship. The house we'd bought needed minor repairs, and the workers we hired seemed much less efficient than those we'd known, perhaps because in the mountains every outdoor job has to be fitted into a much smaller window of suitable weather. The quality of the work here is more elegant but less solid. It was our first clue that by comparison with northern New Hampshire, this was a land of milk and honey. It demonstrated a truth that time had dulled for us, that life in the mountains is harsh as well as beautiful. Pay the price of harshness and you get to live in the beauty.

• •

I've been amused recently at how I'll start to tell friends the intended punchline of the New Hampshire piece—about the discovery of air—and then clam up. I don't want to spoil it by blurting it out before I get it worded right. It's not the most profound observation ever uttered, but it is giving me secret pleasure. Can't wait to write it into the piece.

• •

C. and I drive back up to Easton for a little more concentrated research. While she visits her buddy Ruth, I walk up Coppermine, an AMC trail that leads two and a half miles up the side of Kinsman Ridge to Bridal Veil Falls. On the flat before the trail starts its ascent, there is old-growth white pine that looks big enough for masts for the king: twenty-four inches on the stump, twenty-four yards tall, the minimum standard (as I just read in *Tall Trees*). The flats also contain an ugly new housing development called Coppermine Village. Cutting down coniferous forest leaves a truly hideous scar. I wonder how long it'll take this area to recover and turn into nice woods again.

The vegetation is mostly spruce and white pine before the trail starts to rise. Lots of bird life, but there's something mean and sharp about this understory forest, inhospitable. It doesn't have the lush acceptance of soft-skinned human beings that the Berkshire forests back in Massachusetts seem to have. Twenty minutes in, I come across patches of solid ice in the trail—thirty days before the summer solstice.

If I'm going to get anything useful out of this, it'll have to be a kind of "may I take you along on this walk?" insert. Not exactly a new device, but it made a successful chapter in *On Mountains*. I'd better figure out how to characterize what is so mean about these woods. It's mostly just the scratchy, thorny appearance, I think; conifers put out so many limbs, particularly at the top, and when they go down—and there are a lot of blow-downs—they make a jumbled mass of spiky ladders. They're not actually thorns, but that's the visual effect. One gets the same impression of the dead understory limbs of living trees. Tough stuff.

A couple of days ago we watched a film about a young man making a solo canoe trip across Canada's Barrenlands, and scenes from that adventure keep playing in my head. It makes me very conscious of the need not to sprain an ankle while I'm out here alone.

• •

As I climb, the forest opens up into hardwoods that are just beginning to bud out. A garden: soft, woodsy hillsides with a crashing brook in the middle. Just below the falls there's a small lean-to built by the AMC. Graffito: "We changed the river." Terrific; did you put it back the way you found it?

The waterfall is as spectacular as I remembered, a thin plume that drops thirty feet or so, collects in a small pool, then spills out of that and pours down over a smooth, rounded granite sheet for sixty feet or more to another pool. I once fell and slid the length of that granite sheet. It was the first time I walked up here, with my three kids and C., in 1969.

We were looking for a swimming hole, and splashed and waded in the lower pool, but it wasn't large enough. We climbed to the base of the aerial part of the falls, looking for deeper water; nothing swimmable there, either, so we started back down. Alongside the running water, lush moss covers the granite sheet. I thought I'd inch over onto the wet moss and see if I couldn't just gently and gradually slide down the face of the sheet. I could, but not gradually: the instant I was in the slippery moss I was on my way to the bottom, in the next thing to a free-fall. I'd started out in a squatting position, and somehow, luckily, kept my bare feet under me. Occasional bumps in the surface would send me momentarily flying, but I kept coming back down on my feet and my seat, and continued sliding. I fetched up in the small pool at the bottom of the granite sheet, unhurt but frightened out of my wits. The kids and C. may have been even more frightened than I was—but once we'd discovered the granite's slideability, we spent the next half hour climbing partway up the face and sliding back down into the pool, until we'd worn the seats out of all our pants.

The event became something of a family legend. Now, looking from the bottom, it doesn't look like much of a slide at all. But I climb back up to the top, to approximately the point at which I'd made my original mistake, and it is just as scary as I remembered. This time I work my way back down again very carefully, well to the side of the slippery moss.

So: here I am earning my living by walking in the woods, in a beautiful forest, beside a beautiful stream, on a nice day. I have succeeded in reminding myself what glories hide away on this mountainside. I pause to eat the light lunch in my day pack, then head back down to the car.

• •

Home from New Hampshire to great news from Viking: by mid-April they'd shipped forty-two hundred copies of *Stone Work* to the chains. "Very good," said the editor who sent the news, "for a book that defies categories."

• •

I just realized that the Easton Valley is the geography of my dreams. Our old house there figures frequently in my dreams. In these dreams, as in reality, it's in a broad, gentle, north–south valley, on the east side of the road, up against the wall of mountains. In the dreams everything else may be changed, other houses and barns may be in the wrong place, sometimes the creek behind the house is a large river, but our house is always in the correct place, on the east side of the road. At the head of the valley, to the north, there is even in my dreams a small town (Franconia), with a larger town slightly to the west (Littleton). To the south is a big plug of a mountain (Moosilauke). To the north, beyond Franconia, is nothing but more wildness and mystery, and loneliness.

• •

Meanwhile, back in my waking life, I'm getting a little crazed. There's all this crap stacking up—the piece for Whittle, trying to keep the *Log* on schedule, all these notes and the magazine piece to be made out of them, the work in my head that hasn't gotten down onto paper. And the travel, and social life, and summer about to accelerate the garden and the yard, all that physical labor to get done. It feels uncontrollable. This is what too much of the writing trade seems to be about: processing all this material, getting things shaken into place

so you can get to work again. It is what I have to defend
against. Yes, I have to go do that other stuff from time to
time, but this, here—these pages, this work—is what I'm after.

· ·

Gray Saturday, no rain, bugs beginning to emerge.
Opened my office window yesterday for the first time this
spring.

Perhaps I was sweating over the Whittle piece: I told them
yesterday that I thought I could get it to them Monday, but
I'm still not sure how. Woke up thinking about it during the
night, got on it this morning and in about two hours got it
close. I *think* it's licked.

But mostly I'm excited today about the breakthrough on
the New Hampshire piece: Easton and the geography of
dreams. The geography of dreams, the discovery of air.

· ·

Our woods are really filling in, greening up nicely: it's
paradise except for the bugs, which are out in earnest. This
morning's chill has them slightly discouraged, thank goodness.
C. took her coffee out on the deck, and I wish I'd had the
leisureliness of spirit to join her.

I didn't walk the loop yesterday because I got up at five-
fifteen, worked on the Whittle piece until eight, fetched the
Sunday papers and had breakfast, started prepping the tractor
at ten-thirty, got two thirds of the lawn mowed—and then
stopped in my tracks to go back up and work on Whittle again.
Crazed. This morning I got directly onto it, finished it, Express
Mailed it to Knoxville.

· ·

Photographer Tobey showed up before 6:00 a.m. to shoot the pond; he's working on a feature for *NEM* about ponds, text to be supplied by C.

This morning's mail brought a copy of the contract letter for the New Hampshire piece, which says it was due at the magazine yesterday! Todd and I must have negotiated that due date, and then I forgot about it. The piece isn't scheduled until the November issue, so this is an embarrassment but not an emergency. I sent word to Todd that it'll be ten days late.

So I spent the morning collapsing notes—cutting, compressing, putting things in their proper order. A laborious process, but it probably pays off: it forces me to go through everything and find out what works as writing and what doesn't. I should be able to nail the piece together quickly once that's done.

• •

The idea that dreams have a geography would never have occurred to me if I hadn't started working on this piece, if I hadn't gone back up there trying to discover why that place has such a hold on me. The thing about the geography of dreams is that I'm pretty well certain that geography is the same for everyone else who lives in the valley. Maybe that's the definition of a true compatriot: someone whose dreams have the same geography as your own.

• •

Now, finally, I start back into the piece proper, picking up after the lead: the geology of the White Mountains is well known (or well guessed at, geology being a science of inference), four hundred million years ago yatata-yatata, but the Ice Age is when it starts getting interesting; then what the Ice

Age did to that ridge, smoothing it out, leaving that thin layer
of gravel that New Hampshiremen, unfamiliar with anything
more fertile, call "soil."

One of the things I'm struggling with is this business of
mountain climate. It *is* a mountain climate, those are mountain
villages, but the valley floor is only a thousand feet above sea
level and that hardly seems mountainous. A mountain village
ought to be at six or seven thousand feet, as in Colorado.
When we lived in Easton I'd have been embarrassed to claim
I lived in a mountain village. But that's what it is, and would
be even if it were at sea level, because it is in mountain weather
systems, with mountain soils and all those other mountainous
considerations. On top of the purely latitudinal aspects of the
climate, there's also the fact that Easton is down in a valley,
further reducing the sunlight. To reduce the amount of available light at that latitude is effectively to move miles farther
north—or to move up in altitude.

That's because of Hopkins's Bioclimatic Law, one of the
best things Dr. Jones had to tell me. According to Hopkins,
spring approaches from the south, and fall comes down from
the north, at the rate of four days per degree of latitude. A
degree of latitude is sixty-nine miles, so spring and fall approach at seventeen and a quarter miles per day. Also, the
seasons don't just march up and down the globe: they march
up and down mountainsides too. A degree of latitude is equivalent to a hundred and twenty-two meters of altitude, and vice
versa. Hopkins's law thus draws a kind of X-Y axis in space;
where the lines of altitude and latitude intersect is the true,
as opposed to the calendar, season. These numbers are sometimes rounded off to an annual fifteen miles or one hundred
feet of altitude per day, but this can be misleading. Change
is more gradual in winter and summer. That's why Jones used

the word "steeper" when he compared spring and fall to the rest of the year.

One question I need to resolve is how something as hard as mountain life can also be so soft. That's what I was trying to get at in the note about vividness: if you don't like a certain vividness in your relationship with the natural world, you won't make it in a New England mountain village. In any mountain village.

• •

Scattered clouds, seventy-four degrees, our first summer-like day. God, May is beautiful. Supposed to hold for the next two days. New Hampshire now at twenty-five hundred words, but much too loose. Rigorous tightening to do.

• •

The organizing process has ground to a halt. I had this fantasy of turning all five files into workable pieces of prose, then just mixing and matching the whole thing together. But my faith in organization, otherwise known as a deep-seated need to keep shuffling things around, has finally worn out; I've thrown up my hands and started working on the piece straight through. Still, massaging those files, working so redundantly, familiarized me with the material, and it's going together fast. I pushed ahead fifteen hundred words this morning; those fifteen hundred won't stand up, but five hundred or so of them will. Maybe eight hundred.

Right now I'm looking for a transition into the notes about mountain climate. After I mention the extreme cold when we visited last February, I'll talk about Hopkins's Bioclimatic Law. That bit of "science" will lead into the mountain life. Then I'll put in the story of the town meeting—the gun and the badge—and the existing kicker (the geography of dreams), and, with a few more stories scattered here and there, that's the piece. Then all I have to do is cut it all by two thirds. And then go back and make the sentences work.

· ·

Every bump and knob in your field of vision demonstrates air. It's only when those interruptions give you a sense of distance—draw you out of your own little self-involved cocoon of space—that they begin to articulate the air. We call those views breathtaking; maybe we ought to call them breath-giving.

As I was driving home with the mail this morning, a red-winged blackbird flew across the road in front of me and landed in a roadside white pine. Its flight was a gentle horizontal *S*: a swoop up, a beat of the wings over the top of a convex arc, a slight dive for speed to carry to the landing site, and a flare at the end for the landing. The pleasure of writing is in seeing that lazy *S* take shape in the air, and then trying to describe it—so maybe someone else can see it too, in the mind. The pleasure of looking at nature is the same.

· ·

A glorious summer day, the third in a row. Night before last was a friend's eightieth birthday party, and it was warm enough at sundown to sit outside for drinks. I drove home from Greenfield yesterday with the windows down. Today the pond begins to look inviting.

Tobey showed up to take more pictures at dawn this morning, setting up his tripod on the deck, catching C. in the tub with the shades up. I had no idea that anyone could lie that low in a bathtub.

He showed us some of the slides he's taken, once again demonstrating that photographers see a more beautiful world than I do. Why can't I learn to see like that?

. .

Whittle piece accepted, check on the way.

. .

New Hampshire is coming along nicely, at about three thousand words (of a forty-five-hundred-word max). I'm still struggling with mountain climate. It rains a lot in that valley, forty inches a year. The six weeks going into winter and the six weeks coming out of it can be somewhat monothematic. Monochrome, monotone. Monosyllabic. There is coldness, darkness, isolation, yes, all of that, but it is not a dull existence. Nature has ways of compensating; there are good parts, although they are not easy to characterize. Summer is glorious (despite the bugs); it comes on so hard, for lack of time, that the landscape seems to spew greenness. Fall, of course, is paradisiacal. In winter, stepping out of doors on a forty-below night is one of life's more spellbinding experiences; you almost expect to hear the stars crack open.

. .

Danger sign: I find myself writing a letter to Todd in my head, explaining what I've done. I know I'm working badly when in off moments I find myself writing a letter to explain why a piece is the way it is.

I'm within a couple of hundred words of finishing a first draft—twelve hundred words overlength.

. .

Scarlet tanager at the top of the pasture.

. . . .
. .

New Hampshire is now a solid piece but needs reorganizing; I'll print off a paper copy next, and work on it in that form. One of the more shocking events in electronic writing will then occur. I'll have the text as close to perfect as I think I can get it, will think it ready to send. Then the paper copy will expose how awkward and unfinished it really is. Going from the screen to paper represents a huge change—and therefore a large opportunity for rewriting.

My problem is that I go over the material so many times I memorize it, and am lulled to sleep by my own voice. I can't see the writing anymore, when the whole job of rewriting is to see it fresh. To break through this hypnosis, I sometimes read the pages out of order, even read the sentences in reverse order—from the bottom of the page up—just to jar myself out of this overfamiliarity.

This is in the category of neurotic tricks. C.'s brother, *New Yorker* satirist Bruce McCall, used to claim he needed a certain coarse yellow copy paper because it was the only surface that properly accepted the ink from the typewriter keys. There's one writer who is alleged to type his manuscripts on a speechwriter's typewriter, in letters three quarters of an inch tall, then tape the pages on the wall of his office and proofread with binoculars from across the room. I'm sure that longhand writers feel they squeeze the sentences out of the end of a pencil. Writing is definitely a physical process for me, even with computers; I still have to do a certain amount of keyboarding—*re*keyboarding—to get a grip on a piece.

But then I tend toward the compulsive. I used to write a column for *Esquire,* and by chance started one with an empty wastebasket. When, a week later, I had finished a seven-and-a-half-page manuscript and finally emptied the wastebasket, I counted eighty-seven discarded pages.

That's about the same ratio as in filmmaking, ten or eleven feet of film exposed for every one used. It is not easy to sell that ratio or that working method to students who are writing term papers, or engineers or scientists—or educators or bureaucrats—who are writing reports. It is a ratio, now that I think of it, that one can afford only for projects for which the writing is more important than the information.

But therein may be the definition of a writer. As a writer I don't want to be remembered, or noticed, for the story I thought up or the information I presented, I want to be remembered for how I said it. That's where the ego comes in.

Some of us want to present it so easily you don't know you're getting it.

• •

A certain plunge into gloom along about here. I finished a draft of the New Hampshire piece that was only four hundred words too long, convinced myself it was done, and asked C. to read it. She, diplomatically but obviously, didn't like it. She raised some critical issues about it, mostly having to do with the treatment of people, which throw doubts on some of my deeper insecurities as a writer, my inability to connect, my resistance to prying: my failure to do the basic journalistic job. I have a large wall to climb on this one.

• •

Took a Memorial Day weekend break, then got back to work on the New Hampshire piece. I'd done it in a succession of short takes separated by space breaks, with very little attempt at transitions between them. This seemed to work for me but didn't for C. I took out the breaks, ran paragraphs together, removed the bumpiness. That and a little reorga-

nizing made it remarkably more coherent. It's interesting to
me that the beginning and ending came to me before I wrote
the middle. Not, I think, a good way to work.

Anyway, I finished a draft of the New Hampshire piece
that C. likes, that will go to Todd. Mostly what I'm feeling
is relief—but I do have to plunge ahead into the *Running
Log*.

• •

Magazine writing has been an interesting reimmersion.
Whittle offered a remarkable eighteen hundred dollars for
twelve hundred words—essentially, a double *Running Log*—
so I grabbed it. Did a first draft in two days, quickly calculating
how much I'd make if I could keep that up (nine hundred
dollars a day, forty-five hundred a week, eighteen thousand
a month, two hundred sixteen thousand per year). Then fiddled around with it three or four more days, trying to get it
right. Finally, after eight working days, I sent it off—and re-
calculated my projected annual income on that basis. I knew
it wasn't quite right yet, though, and asked for guidance, which
I got, which sent me back for another three or four days, and
at some point in there I realized that I'd been demoted from
two hundred thousand a year to about eighteen thousand,
and if this kept up I'd be in the poorhouse.

Similarly, the New Hampshire piece: I got swept up in it,
over-researched it, overwrote it, had twenty thousand words
of notes for a forty-five-hundred-word piece. I ended up putting thirty-two working days into it—and twelve such pieces
a year, if I could possibly keep up that pace, wouldn't pay a
decent year's salary.

But it was something I loved writing, powerful material—
for me, anyway—that I wanted to get down. Not a bad deal,

really. The only hard part was sitting here and watching it eat the days.

• •

During my first twenty years or so of magazine writing I had no working method at all. On most interviews I'd try just to go through the experience, paying as much attention as I could, and then, later, write the piece from memory. That worked fairly well, but I didn't realize how insulted the subjects were that I took no notes. When I finally did start taking notes—to ease their fears—I found the process of note-taking got in the way of paying attention. I never did solve that one.

My journalism was only of the most superficial variety anyway. The true job of journalism, getting the story of what happened or happens, is an almost gymnastic task, a fascinating discipline at its highest level. At my level it was a completely irritating one, seeming to have nothing to do with writing, at least in the way that I practiced it. Of course it was on the most trivial of subjects, and the part I enjoyed most was the most trivial (but most dramatic) aspect of those subjects: racing, of cars, on skis, in athletics. These may be appropriate human activities, but never struck me, even when I was participating in them, as the sort of thing to which a grown-up ought to be devoting his time.

In *For Love & Money* Jonathan Raban talks about the practice of journalism:

A few days spent in someone else's world (however dismal, violent, pretty or even boring that world may be) is simply not enough to experience it as real. It is too tightly framed by one's own domestic normality. Wherever you are today, you know that next Monday you will be home, and from the perspective of home today will seem too exaggerated, too highly coloured, too remote to take quite seriously. So the writer slips into a style of mechanical facetious irony as he deals with this wrong-end-of-the-telescope view of the world. The perfervid similes that are the trademark of the hardened magazine writer betray him as he tries to make language itself mask and make up for the fundamental shallowness of his experience with its synthetic energy. . . . Emotional disengagement, self-conscious observation, the capacity to quickly turn a muddle of not very deeply felt sensations into a neat and vivid piece, are part of the necessary equipment of the writer as journalist.

• •

Pause to reread *Stone Work* quickly in book form, to get a sense of how it reads now that it's between covers. One startling rediscovery is that there is almost no reason ever to put anything in italics. Why can't I *remember* that? And there are still some commas I'd like to remove.

. . . the worst of writing is that one depends so much upon praise. —Virginia Woolf

J U N E

• • • • • • • • • • • • • • • • • • • •

On the loop this morning the dogs came across a grouse with babies; the mother went immediately into the broken-wing act, fluttering back and forth across the trail right under my feet, just out of the reach of Molly's chomping mouth. Meanwhile the dozen or fifteen chicks disobeyed all instructions, running around crazily and peeping at the top of their lungs. I managed to get both dogs past the whole scene with no harm done. For the next twenty yards the mother kept trying to lure us away—performing, it occurred to me later, as a rodeo clown. Wonderful scene. Hello, June.

The loop that we walk is a little less than a mile and a half of old logging roads and connecting paths, gaining and giving back about seven hundred feet of altitude over its course. It starts—or ends, depending on your direction—with a rugged uphill climb, almost to the height of land, then cuts directly across the sidehill for four or five hundred yards, crosses a couple of small brooks, swings through an old sawmill site,

116

then follows a mostly buried granite ridge down to pasture
level, where it circles back to the foot of the pond behind our
house. It winds through mixed hardwood, white pine and
hemlock forest, parts of which were logged off thirty years
ago—thus the sawmill—and have grown back blowsy and ill
defined.

The woods it winds through are habitat for deer, turkey,
grouse, pheasant, quail, coyote, porcupine, skunk, rabbit, rac-
coon, beaver, probably possum and mink, songbirds in great
numbers, and more than one bear. One sees a lot of fiery
orange efts in the path—and, in the pond below, the olive-
drab newt, which I've been told is the amphibious mode of
the same creature. Also in the pond are large- and smallmouth
bass, minnows, frogs, tadpoles, several billion smaller, more
or less microscopic creatures, and, above it, dragonflies. Owls.
Lots of owls in the woods, several different owl calls reverberating at dusk, the birds that make them almost never seen.
Bugs that don't bite and bugs that do. Ferns—a principal
feature of the woods is ferns. Portions of the woods are in-
fested with wild grape, which threatens to pull down trees;
foresters tell us the only cure is chemical, and we haven't had
the resolve to take that harsh step. The hillside holds an enormous amount of water—including the water supply for our
house and four or five more down the valley—and the trail
is often wet. The loop is at its glorious best when the woods
are wet too, after a rain, every surface washed down and fresh,
the colors vibrant, the dust settled. In spring it is an achingly
light and airy arboretum, in summer an enchanted green tun-
nel, in autumn a stained-glass gothic cathedral. I like it best
in wintertime, on snowshoes, but then it's no longer a loop,
it's just terrain, a vast hillside of swooping hummocks and
hollows, hills and dales, allowing you to go anywhere you like.

It is alive with birdsong and trickling water, from the snowmelt of very early spring right through to the annual August drought. In the fall the wildlife goes wacky, and you're apt to see anything. In winter, with a coat of snow, it is Disney-fied, neatened up. In spring it is clarified.

"A thing is right when it tends to preserve the integrity, stability, and beauty of the biotic community," wrote Aldo Leopold. "It is wrong when it tends otherwise." I think I do no harm to the loop by walking it. I don't help it either. It helps me instead, and I like to think that I'm part of the biotic community, too. Walking it is the best thing I do. Besides, the dogs need it so.

• •

Finished another *Log* today, the start of a hard drive to get them all done and out of here.

The idea for this one came to me during a single circuit of the loop, and I dictated it in something close to finished form as I walked. I'm beginning to get the rhythm back. Recently I made a note to myself about the *but*-paragraph, and realized that, having done so many of these little essays (sixteen per year for six years, now), I'm also beginning to get the form nailed down. By "but-paragraph" I mean the on-the-other-hand part of the essay, the antithesis to its thesis, strophe to its antistrophe: a few remarks, not necessarily limited to a single paragraph, that shine a slightly different light on the basic premise. The essays often seem to fall naturally into something of a call-and-response structure, almost sonnetlike. There will be an octet (four hundred words of basic premise), a quatrain (two hundred words of but-paragraph), and a couplet (a kicker—a line or two of joke, a reference back to the lead, a connector to the overarching theme of the piece). I didn't have this structure in mind when I made the note, and didn't know what to call the second element. "But-paragraph" was the term that came bubbling up as if it were common in the language. I'd never heard it called that, but I've used the term since with other writers and they seem to get what I mean.

This implies a much firmer grasp of structure than I really have. You don't write a six-hundred-word essay by saying you'll write four hundred words about this, two hundred words about that, and tack a kicker on the end; you just make the argument. You do the best job you can of explicating the subject, saying what you have to say about it. The form grows out of the material, the material isn't fitted to the form. Maybe this is what Chomsky is saying about our brains being hard-wired for grammar: it is the syntax—the deep grammar—of the idea that generates its form. You never have to think of form, in fact it is probably safer not to; only in the later re-writes, at the stage when you're having trouble making the piece work, is there any point in thinking about form at all. Editors don't think in those terms either. The editor reads the piece to see if it works; if it doesn't, the editor will try, or ask the writer to try, to fix it so it does. But it's not fixing it to fit the form, it is fixing it to be more effective.

C. and I discuss these matters in the June dusk. She points out that birdsong, too, usually takes the form of call-and-response. Maybe that's the way all language works.

• •

Library Journal says *Stone Work* is ". . . likely to be important as Annie Dillard's *Pilgrim at Tinker Creek* and Tracy Kidder's *House*." I read the review at the post office, bring it home and hand it to C. with a poker face. Then I reread it over her

. . . .

shoulder, and as we come to that line I grab her at the waist and start bouncing—bouncing her, bouncing myself, bouncing us both up and down around the kitchen, both of us laughing dementedly.

• •

Spent the morning reading old runner's magazines, cleaning the accumulated stack of them off my desk, pulling clips for ideas for future *Log*s.

I am still essentially ecstatic from yesterday's *Library Journal*, now referred to around the house as "likely as important." C. has taken to calling me "Likely." I am stunned by that piece of good fortune. Four out of five of the bellwethers (sales to chains, Book-of-the-Month Club, *Kirkus*, *Library Journal*) have been positive, and the fifth—*Publishers Weekly*—not in yet. Then the real reviews will start. If it gets reviewed.

• •

Win some, lose some: *Booklist*, another source of capsule reviews, panned *Stone Work*. Someone there really didn't like it: ". . . Jerome wants to get down to some deep, meaning-of-life-type stuff, and fans of his writing will probably think he succeeds. (Other readers may find him too tediously groovy for words.)"

It's an amusingly mean little paragraph, and I laughed about it on the way home from the post office—feeling all the while as if I'd met with physical violence. If I were doing one-paragraph book reviews I'd probably do them nastily too, just to get some jokes in, catch the reader's attention. But this time makes me think I'll never write another negative review.

I expect the book to strike a certain percentage of readers as unnecessarily self-involved, and this is the first of those

readers I've heard from. I've instructed C. to stop calling me
Mr. Likely; henceforth I am to be referred to as Old Tediously
Groovy.

. .

Todd liked the New Hampshire piece and has already put
through the request for the check: great news financially, also
a relief because it means the piece doesn't need substantial
work and is therefore closer to being out of my hair, not to
absorb any more writing time.

There is one minor frustration connected with the news. I
signed up to do the piece in the first place because Dick Todd
has such a good reputation as an editor, and C. has had a long
succession of enlightening experiences working with him. I
had the ulterior motive of seeing what I could learn about
magazine writing from a master editor. If he likes the piece
as is, I miss that chance. Of course I must also assume that
when he gets around to editing the piece for the magazine,
I'll get the chance to work it over at his direction. I'm not
ready to assume that it does not need work.

. .

In the best writing, there is a strong sense of inevitability
to each sentence as it comes. Given this sentence, the next
sentence is the one that must inevitably follow. One almost
says, Oh, of course, that's exactly what would have to be said
next. It is a confirmation of what you've begun to understand
from the piece of writing.

But at the same time there has to be a little surprise in the
sentence, a little twist that takes you somewhere just slightly
unexpected. E. B. White is the master of this: "I go to church
once in a while and sing the hymns very loud; it clears the

blood, and I love the gush of holiness when the old bone-shaking anthems ripple up and down my spine and crackle in my larynx."

• •

My thirteen free author's copies of *Stone Work* have arrived; now comes the somewhat tender job of figuring out the most appropriate thirteen people to send them to—starting with family, of course. Also, National Public Radio called to set up an interview. I'm eager to do it; Noah Adams is a skilled and comfortable interviewer, and an appearance on NPR does more for a book than just about any other medium short of the major talk shows.

There are other radio talk shows that are not so pleasant. I did one once, plugging a sports book, over what might be called an 800-number station, or talk-show factory. They scheduled me for an hour, then kept me on hold while they finished up an extra twenty minutes of call-ins from co-dependency enthusiasts and battered wives describing their most recent beatings. The program broke every seven minutes or so for three one-minute commercials selling investment schemes, mineral supplements, itch ointments, and other snake oils, each ending with an 800 number for ordering the product. My hosts were an entirely too perky couple who specialized in talking like real people, playing hard to the late-night lonelies.

No calls came in for my segment. I'm sure this confirmed their market research, ensuring that no further jock books would be promoted over their airtime. That view is probably right; I can't imagine anyone who might be interested in my books listening to such a program. But when books disappear so easily into the great abyss, when only some miracle gives a book a market shelf life longer than, in Calvin Trillin's im-

mortal phrase, a quart of milk, one does not pass up oppor-
tunities for promotion.

When T. George Harris started *American Health,* he put me
on the masthead as a contributing editor. (I'd written the cover
piece for the premiere issue.) I knew this meant only that I'd
be given some kind of vague favored-writer status for future
assignments, but asked anyway if there were some kind of
reward connected with this lofty honor. "Well, we can't pay
you anything," T. George said, "but I like to think of the
printing press as a kind of prayer wheel. When it's spinning
out pages with your name on them, it has to be doing you
some good, doesn't it?"

· ·

C. finished and mailed her proposal to agent Don Congdon. Our fingers are crossed.

· ·

Writerliness: I used to have a blithe confidence in my lyrical skills. I had something of a reputation for it; editors called
me when a subject demanded a little poetry. I could always
wax lyrical, about anything, any time I wanted to. I was always
willing to stop and sing. Over time that solution has come to
seem less and less appropriate. I can't justify it anymore, can't
afford it somehow. Describing just to be descriptive has no
point. If I think of a passage that I am writing as descriptive,
it is guaranteed to fail. If I work instead at putting the reader
in the place, taking the reader through the experience, it may
have a chance at working. But it still makes me nervous.

· ·

This is a wonderfully excruciating time. The good news
continues to roll in about *Stone Work,* C. and I are both in a

phase of very high productivity, and . . . we're broke. The checks keep not coming in, not coming in. I've tried to break the habit, but the trip to the post office remains my most pressing daily duty. Freelances live and die by the mail.

I expect my mail to improve shortly. *Stone Work* is a book that old friends might conceivably read—the first of those in a long time, since I've been writing category books, and old friends aren't likely to read category books. So this one is a message, saying, Hey, folks, this is what I've been up to for the past four or five years.

• •

An acquaintance sends a (mercifully) short manuscript for comment; unfortunately, he's been bitten by the desktop-publishing bug, and it is an almost unreadable graphic hodgepodge. He's used a terrible (but "elegant") typeface and lots of italics (in a typeface smaller than the body text), great blaring boldface crossheads, the pages single-spaced with flush right and left margins. It is as if he's done as much as he could to thwart the reader. One can't help suspecting that he's disguising the essential emptiness of the contents. As in most academic writing.

In the early days of electronic writing my younger brother, Dan, sent a letter printed with flush right and left margins. To fill the lines, the software had thrown in an occasional arbitrary extra space between some of the words. "Reading this must be like having a date with a gap-toothed girl," he said. "You never see her pretty smile for staring at the space between her teeth."

It's a powerful observation. Reading is movement, and the spaces as well as the words have meaning. Gratuitous spaces stop and start the eye; reading text printed that way is like driving a car with square wheels. Such text only exists because word-processing software is created not by writers but by engineers. If they can devise a method to give you flush margins, by golly that's what they'll give you, and readability can go hang. The first thing a professional writer does with new software is disable the flush-right-margin feature. Manuscripts should be printed flush left and ragged right, because that's what a professional editor is accustomed to seeing and will therefore be least distracted by. The writer wants the editor paying attention to the thinking, not to the spaces between and around the words.

The second thing a writer does with new software is format for manuscript: eight-and-a-half- by eleven-inch pages, double spaced, with an inch of margin at top, bottom, and on both sides, with an identifying slug-line at the top and a consistent page-numbering system. The idea is to make the physical manuscript as invisible as possible. All those graphic gimmicks so beloved of desktop fans are positive hindrances to an editor.

I'm amazed at how many would-be writers get led into this particular folly. I've seen pieces of writing—usually early experiments with new software—printed in vertical columns ten characters wide, with four or five columns to the page. (The most readable line of type is one and a half times as long as a complete alphabet in the typeface used.) I've yet to see a graphic design by an amateur that improves on the standard typescript format. The most offensive mistake is the use of mismatched fonts, sprinkled with hyperemphatic boldface in place of effective writing. It's antireading.

. .

The *Stone Work* print order was 11,500—not a huge vote of confidence, but okay—of which a little over eight thousand have been shipped. Official pub date is 7/3: this book will be born on the third of July.

The deflating effect of that *Booklist* review has at least stopped my fantasies about how the book is going to change my life. (Those grapes are probably sour anyway.) Now comes a complete surprise: I'm reading the *Boston Globe* and my book-jacket photo jumps out at me; here's an early review by Bob MacDonald, quite favorable. Lose some, win some.

• •

Finished the last *Log*, then read the whole set straight through. I'd done the last five hurriedly, and was worried that they wouldn't hold up. They do. It's been a particularly satisfying bout of production, and is ready to mail.

Then I get to resume my own work. I've taken off two months to do Their work, now I get to do My work. The point of this exercise is to be able to do My work all the time.

• •

Back when I was making a living entirely from magazines, a young woman with a fresh M.A. came to me for advice. She was torn between journalism and teaching. "What I want to know is," she said, "in these magazine articles that you write, do you get to, like, *express* yourself?"

I sputtered some lame answer about that not mattering—irritated that she should ask, that I couldn't answer clearly, that there was no simple way to say how badly the question missed the point. In some way I've been sputtering ever since. What I was trying to say to her was that the moment one loses sight of getting it said, of telling the story in the most effective way one can, is the moment the writing goes bad. Funny that her question should have caught me off guard: a couple of years before, when I taught my first and only writing class, the course description had said "no self-expression allowed." But nobody had paid any attention to that anyway.

Not that there's much point in worrying over it. While you're writing—unless you're far better at it than I am—the analytical part of your mind is doing everything it can to get the story told or the scene described or whatever the objective of the piece is. You're hanging by your fingernails, just trying to get the thing down in halfway comprehensible fashion. But while that's going on, the rest of your brain is in there at the old Wurlitzer, doing riffs, humming melodies, tossing up tunes for you to try out. Making little suggestions, nudges toward getting the sentence to balance, to have a little ring to it. You think you're spending all your time and energy just trying to get the damned story told, but at the same time you're doing this other thing, playing with the music. It is not your ego intruding but your better sense, trying to make your sentences work more effectively. If you succeed, the question of self-expression will never come up.

• •

Most of the loop is a single path down the middle of a wider clearing, but here and there I can still make out the twin paths of what I like to imagine were wagon wheels, although they were probably logging trucks. Where I can discern the double path I picture farm wagons rolling over it, and a life lived at a walking pace. (Anything faster would shake your teeth out, would break the wheels of your wagon.) Somehow the places where you can see two paths connote a walking pace more strongly than where only the single footpath remains.

A walking pace seems infinitely desirable these days. Why

don't we all just get together and agree to it, junk the fax and all the other technological gadgets for compressing time? Such a foolish dream: we'd work as fast as we can with or without the technology. I do, always, at everything. I wish I didn't. I wash dishes as fast as I can, I write as fast as I can. I am a rapid but sloppy typist (and the sloppiness has been exacerbated by the ease of correction of electronic writing). I read as fast as I can, which made me give up on poetry forty years ago. When I slow down my concentration fades.

I keyboard voluminous notes and various other material, building huge files that I seldom use. I seem to absorb material only by whisking over the top of it, again and again and again, hoping some small percentage of it will adhere each time through.

But the real reason for this hyperkinetic pounding away at the machine is, I fear, a fluttery, superficial, inch-deep involvement in the world. I am utterly busy saving time for the saving of it, nothing more. Sometimes I think the only time I can slow down is when I walk the loop.

· ·

Started fiddling with the New Hampshire piece again, couldn't keep my hands off it. I have a revision in mind, and actually started doing it, but decided to let it rest: if I'm not careful there'll be two versions floating around, and everybody, including myself, will get confused. But I can't get it out of my mind, keep going back to it. Can't leave it alone, keep having the feeling I haven't done it yet. Haven't done it well enough yet.

Actually, a rough idea for a next book has been forming in my mind, springing directly out of the New Hampshire piece, connecting also with a memoir that my brother Jud is

writing. In his memoir Jud talks briefly of the fishing trips
that we used to make with our parents to the Kiamichi Mountains of southeastern Oklahoma, back in the thirties and early
forties. We always stayed with a Cherokee family, the Wards,
who ran a "tourist court"—really a subsistence farm with a
couple of extra roadside cabins—on the banks of the Mountain Fork River. Those trips always served a dual purpose: to
go fishing, which was one of my father's passions, and to get
close to the Arkansas border and legal booze, instead of the
bootleg stuff he drank at home in Oklahoma City—drink being
the other of my father's passions. These trips were what you
would call rich experiences.

Richer for me, perhaps, than for Jud: the Ward family had
been responsible for forming most of my ideas about woods
and mountains, and Jud's few pages brought memories of my
own swarming to the surface. I began to itch to write about
the Kiamichi Mountains myself, to write my own version. The
New Hampshire piece has seemed to open up new possibilities
in writing about place, and I begin to conceive a book on the
subject: a memoir, really, focusing not on my precious self but
on the places where that self spent important time. The Kiamichis at one end—the keystone of the book, really—and New
Hampshire at the other, the magazine piece fleshed out and
expanded. In between, the piney woods of East Texas, where
I spent the World War II years; the Comal River, a gem of a
clear-water river not far from San Antonio, every inch of which
I swam regularly during my high-school days (the river is only
seven miles long); and the high desert rimrock country west
of the Pecos, where I taught high school in the late 1950s.
Five vastly different landscapes, vastly different terrains, vastly
different lifestyles that resulted. I want to write the best rec-
ollection I can of those places, then go back and look at them

now, thirty or forty or fifty years later, and redraw the picture. Record the changes, see how my perceptions have changed. I even came up with a working title: *The Sky Over That Place.*

But now I'm getting cold feet. It's a lovely project but not exactly a bombshell of a book idea, and I can't imagine a publisher getting very excited about a memoir from a non-celebrity. I doubt it would draw an advance large enough even to support the research, never mind the necessary writing time. As I watch what seems to be happening with *Stone Work,* I figure I'd better seize the momentum from the good reviews and pursue something that's serious but also a little more salable. I'd very much like to write *Place* someday, and vow that I will, but it may not be the next book to do.

· ·

Todd has told C., privately, that he's leaving the magazine to pursue book editing and teaching. I sent him a note this morning insisting that he also find time to write more. Why do I want to infect others with my obsessions?

· ·

Place keeps coming back, coming back into my mind. There's something powerful there—for me, anyway.

To be able to afford to do it, I need to figure out a way to avoid regionalism, or the appearance of regionalism: some way of making the book appeal to people who are interested in things other than Oklahoma, Texas, or New Hampshire. What I want it to be is a book not about a collection of specific regions but about the way we are rooted in the natural world, rooted in ways that we don't ever quite know. It is aimed at exposing these aspects of our rootedness that we never notice.

The concept is colored by rereading Ian Frazier's wonderful

book *The Great Plains.* I wonder if the publishing business considers that a regional book. Its appeal seems to me to be not to people interested in that region but to people interested in good writing. I wonder if booksellers see that—or have much interest in trying to sell books to those people. *A River Runs Through It* isn't about trout fishing, it's about a way of living in the West—a way that has more or less run its course. *Place* will be about how we're rooted in our local physical geography; how we are informed (and formed) by the geography of place. If I say that enough times, in enough different ways, maybe I'll find a way eventually to make it come clear.

· ·

The mail brings a thoughtful letter from old friend Kathy Hewett about *Stone Work.* "I don't quite believe that the Stonework John is just the same as you," she said. "Do you?"

The question rocks me back on my heels. You start with the task of making the reader forget that she is reading—a subterfuge, an initial dishonesty out of which whatever you write is forever trying to climb. You throw up some structure or conceit that you hope will hold the reader's attention long enough for you to say what you want to get said. (Of course you can't come right out and say it: another subterfuge.) You spend your time trying to get each sentence honest—or clear, same thing—in hopes that if the bits are true then what they add up to will hold up. You never quite know what they are going to add up to. You end up always with a tissue of lies, in despair.

I am shaken by the question. If that's not my voice, whose voice can it possibly be?

· ·

· · · · · · · · · · · · · · · ·

C.'s last *NEM* column was about planting trees. People keep coming up to her and telling her how moved they were by it; there is this outpouring of connection, admissions of tears. It makes me realize that C. has lived an extremely rich life—just as everyone else has—and that those riches are still largely unexamined. Just like everyone else's riches. Now, as a relatively skillful writer, she is beginning to tap into those riches. She is of an age to begin discovering and pointing up the universals in her experience; when she does it intelligently and tastefully, those moments connect. Even if they are the most minor details of the story.

C. is much better at this than I am. All my life I've been straining to demonstrate how different I am—when the object of the game, if I can only bear to admit it, is to show how alike we all are. Nobody ever said I was a quick study.

· ·

Kathy's letter has really been working in my mind, shocking me once again with the great variance in reading that different people get out of the same material. Every person reads his or her own book; I always forget that. In *Stone Work* I kept reminding myself to pay better attention to the natural world; Kathy seems to have taken that as a kind of schoolteacherish reprimand: Pay attention, reader! I think she was arguing with it as she read, her back up at being given that useless old piece of advice.

Not that I quarrel with her reading. The work has to stand up to any interpretation the reader gets out of it. But I'm really struck with wonder at how many ways there are to read the same book.

It was a startling letter. No one else among my close friends has ever attempted to initiate that kind of discussion of my work. Except for C., of course. I'm more honored than troubled by it.

. .

C. and I are on a bubble these days. She's waiting for Congdon to tell her what's going on with her proposal, which we assume is making the rounds, and for which she could get an offer at any time. I'm waiting for the fate of *Stone Work* to come clear. The real reviews could begin hitting any day.

This suspended state does bad things to the daily life of the writer. One develops a strange lust for any word from the outside, any reaction. Every day for three or four days I'll hear something about the book and its fate; then a whole day will pass without a word, and I panic: *what's gone wrong?*

It reminds me of an interview with James Clavell, the author of lust-in-the-dust best-sellers set in the Orient. He said that with his first book he'd made this silent bargain with himself: if the book just appeared one time on the *Times* best-seller list, he'd be perfectly satisfied. Then it did, and stayed there for a week or two, and he began making the same bargain: if it would just climb a notch. And so on, to the top, and then for how many weeks it stayed there, and the desolation he felt when it started slipping from the top slot.

Shortly after *In Cold Blood* was published, Truman Capote talked about its launching. You have to do it all in six weeks, he said: do all the promotion, arrange all the publicity, get everything cocked and ready to go on the publication date. (I seem to recall his face on the cover of *Life* during that book's first flurry of attention.) Last spring I had the excruciating experience of watching Willy's six weeks—the beehive of activity, the broadcast of the *Nova* based on the book, the interviews and lectures and public appearances. I watched him crisp on the grill as sales refused to take off. He has now put all that behind him, has gone west this month to begin research on a new book. I am trying desperately to go to school on his six weeks, and not succeeding. I am unable to keep myself from fantasies about how to spend the money the book is unlikely to make.

So C. and I walk around bumping into things, unable to concentrate on the work we should be doing, knowing that at any moment the phone may ring with really good (or moderately bad) news; distracted not only from what we do best but from what we enjoy doing most. I was not as sympathetic as I could have been when Willy was going through this. Now the shoe is on my foot. How exquisitely it pinches.

I must say, though, that on my walk today, at the time of year I love the best, on the most glorious day of the summer so far, I am acutely aware that this is the life I've always wanted to arrange for myself. And part of the joy right now is anticipation of the work to be done: the next one, where it goes from here. Am I an optimist? The inscription on my tombstone is going to say, "What's good about *this* is . . ."

• •

Good review in the *L.A. Times* today, more dancing around the kitchen. We decide to go into town, blow off the afternoon. C.'s latest column is done, why not celebrate? We drop by the *NEM* offices and shanghai Todd for lunch; we eat and drink on an outdoor terrace in late June sunshine. Todd says he read *Stone Work* in "three long swallows."

So I'm basking in that, too: I could pick few other people in the business whose respect means more. What a wonderful time this is. June has been delicious. They're haying our fields.

. . . and then the letters, the talk, the reviews, all serve to enlarge the pupil of my mind more and more. I can't settle in, contract, and shut myself off.

—Virginia Woolf

• • • • • • • • • • • • • • • • •

Start of the big holiday weekend—and publication day is Monday, the third. I spend a whirling, spinning Saturday morning getting my desk swept into shape, taking care of bookkeeping and other business-side stuff, then declare my own holiday. This past couple of months has been in violation of my vow—repeated, oh, every two days for the past ten years—to stop hurrying. I spent May and June hurrying, and I wasn't going to do that anymore. I've also gotten off into more stupid fantasies about the future of *Stone Work*. I must keep in mind how small the audience is for a book like that.

••

Dan Okrent, editor of *New England Monthly*, is quietly making plans to leave the magazine at the end of the year. Although most of my recent editorial negotiation has been with Todd, Okrent is the editorial vision behind the magazine, the sensibility that has shaped it from the inception. C. and I have known Dan since 1976, when he was a book editor in New York. He was the second editor (of thirteen) to reject *Truck,* but quickly made up for that, as far as I was concerned, by publishing my next book, *On Mountains,* for Harcourt Brace Jovanovich. He left New York soon thereafter, moved to western Massachusetts, started a book-packaging partnership and edited the very successful *Ultimate Baseball Book,* began writing books of his own. He also helped *Texas Monthly* launch a book division, and in looking at that magazine saw a possibility for New England. So he hooked up with Bob Nylen and began raising money for *NEM.* C., who had done freelance editing for Dan's book-packaging enterprise, was the first employee hired. He's been its editor from the beginning, has established a very fine magazine, but after five years is burnt out. That's inescapable in magazine jobs, I think, if one cares enough to bear the job in the first place.

. .

How to write a book proposal: imagine that the book-to-be gets onto the *Times* best-seller list, then write the two-line summary that would run with its listing. Before you write the proposal, write—in twenty-five words or less—what the book is and why it's on the list. I've never tried it, but it makes sense to me.

It would never have occurred to me, of course, if I weren't at least subconsciously entertaining the foolish notion of an appearance on that list someday by something I wrote.

. .

Publication day. We virtually awoke to a call from C.'s brother Bruce, who read to us Christopher Lehmann-Haupt's review in the daily *New York Times:* totally positive. C. says it's the best review I've ever gotten, and I am not inclined to argue. Spent the rest of the day drifting around on a cloud.

This phone call has become something of a family tradition. Bruce gets his paper early, and he has checked in with first news of a *Times* review five times now, for five different books.

• •

For the second night in a row I awoke at 4:30 a.m. and couldn't go back to sleep for an hour or so. Must be publication of the book. It's all rather baffling, as I don't feel stressed out, can't tell that I'm "suffering" from any disturbance. I don't recall overreacting to pub dates in the past, but C., who has a better memory, says I did. Anyway, this one seems to be registering several points on the old stress meter. Weird: the stress of good news.

• •

Lunch with Willy, which we spent railing at each other about the usual things. He's definitely gathering momentum for his next book project, and it's nice to see. Fire in his eyes. I told him my twenty-five-word blurb approach; he seemed taken with the idea, and asked me at what point I did this. Told him I'd never thought of it before the other night, but suspected it should be as early in the project as possible.

Before and after lunch I tried to work on this manuscript, but spent most of the time daydreaming—and answering the phone, accepting congratulations from various people for the *Times* review, chatting about the wisdom and perspicacity of my good friend Lehmann-Haupt. (I've never met the man.) No new sales figures beyond the original eight thousand. I figure the book will start to move or not on the basis of this review and the National Public Radio interview. *Washington*

Post and the Sunday *Times* are the important reviews still to come.

• •

Paid bills this morning: to cover the mortgage, property taxes, and our current bills requires $26.40 more than we have on hand—unless I clean out a savings account with thirty-two dollars in it. Somehow this does not make me crazy, perhaps because I've decided to stall for a few weeks on the property taxes.

The phone is still ringing, as people see the *Times* review and check in. Warm, funny conversations: one of them, a local friend, started off without a hello, just "I think Lehmann-Haupt is a wonderful writer . . ."

Didn't get any "work" done, in other words, but didn't care. Still in that giddy pub-date state. It was a beautiful blue-white-and-yellow-cumulus day, a lovely day to be outdoors, so I mowed the pond pasture, struck by the realization that the only way I find to spend time on that nice piece of land is to mow it. I should go lie on my back in it and look up at the sky. I don't. Kids do that. I did it as a kid. Why not now? Too itchy?

• •

Stone Work has already gotten a better response than anything else I've written, with the possible exception of *Truck*. I am trying to inoculate myself against the notion that it could be my *Coming into the Country*. There's an alluring and altogether distracting history of writers who publish for years with little recognition, then strike it big. Richard Bach's *Jonathan Livingston Seagull* might be the type example. When I worked at *Car and Driver* we used to get an occasional manuscript from

Bach, a onetime car nut. We never bought anything from him, but I dimly remembered the name—associating it, because of those rejections, with failure—when he hit so incredibly big with *Seagull.*

It is as easy to fall in love with a rich person as a poor one: if one is going to spend all this effort writing books, they might just as well be about things people want to know about. Or, as Annie Dillard put it, in *The Writing Life,* ". . . writing sentences is difficult whatever their subject. It is no less difficult to write sentences in a recipe than sentences in *Moby-Dick.* So you might as well write *Moby-Dick.*"

• •

Stormy day, buckets of rain, but with a strange little midday sunshine break that perfectly accommodated the visit from a reporter for the *Greenfield Recorder,* working on a feature about *Stone Work.* Nice young woman, a pleasant conversation: she asked good questions, had read the book carefully, had a real sense of the place before she got here.

• •

No book news at all today, for the first time since about mid-June. Maybe I can now get my feet back on the ground and get some work done.

I'm thinking about *Place* again. The Kiamichi piece could sell to *Esquire,* or even, cross my fingers, *The New Yorker.* The Gulf Coast, Comal River, and West Texas pieces should sell to *Texas Monthly.* As soon as I get the proposal a little closer, I should pitch them. A couple of good magazine sales would help pay for the research for the book.

One problem with magazine writing is that each piece must pay its own way, buying enough time to get it done. Magazine

writing lives on ideas that take a month to produce (think up,
sell to the editor, research, write, get past the editor again,
revise, pass through fact-checking) and pay about half a
month's expenses. And never build any equity at all. Books
at least hold out the hope of continuing income.

There are thousand-dollar ideas (magazine pieces), thirty-
thousand-dollar ideas (most books that have a chance of succeeding), million-dollar ideas (forget books, these are prop-
erties, marketed rather than written). As publishing now
seems to be constituted, it is the idea and not the execution
that has currency. There are sound reasons why publishing
works this way, but they are the strictures of commerce and
not of good writing. There is something poisonous for the
writer in even thinking of them, but one must. What I need
right now is, oh, a forty-thousand-dollar idea, on which I'll
then try to live and work for the next two years. I won't make
as much as the local route salesman who drives a potato-chip
van, but I probably have a nicer life. I have a sweet deal. I
certainly don't want to do anything else.

Thinking about the sweetness of the deal, however, is of
no help with ideas. I am being confused, as usual, by commerce. Coming up with an idea that solves the economic problem is difficult but not impossible; the harder part is finding
the idea that does that and also compels the writer to write
the book. That's the one thing that every decent book must
have going for it. I've read too many books in which the author
has obviously lost interest two thirds of the way through, and
I deeply fear getting caught in such a project myself. When
I read, as soon as I begin to wonder why the author is bothering to tell me something, I begin to realize that the author
is simply bothering me. This is a sin I would rather not commit,
even for more money than the potato-chip guy makes.

. . . .

• •

If I do the *Place* book, I'll be going back to the Kiamichi Mountains after a fifty-year interlude. My hope would be that fifty years after that someone else might come look at those hills and find my description useful. My record might help someone else describe the changes that have taken place.

That's an interesting reason for the book: to put down a picture of the place useful for future studies. In that sense alone it's worth doing, although a bottom-line publisher might not think so. Maybe a university press would be interested. Not interested enough, I'd imagine, to pay for time to do the work.

• •

The publishing business as benevolent patron: my dream is that *Stone Work* will be the book that pulls me out of this patronage system. I need it to do well enough to establish me as a writer of more than midrange books, of books that do little more than break even.

But I also have this shaky feeling that if *Stone Work* doesn't catch hold, this current manuscript might be the last midrange contract I get. After eight nonsmashes, a publisher is less likely to invest in me as a writer for the future. I am approaching sixty, and still have hopes that my career will not just dwindle to a stop; it is therefore time for things to start clicking. This makes for additional pressure, on top of the usual publishing-day jitters. It surely has something to do with this squirrelly, distracted state I'm in.

• •

My admiration for good editors is unbounded, probably because I was so lousy at the job myself. I caught on to the mechanics quickly enough, but that part of it never captured my interest sufficiently to generate much energy. The writing part always did.

From the writer's point of view, the editor's first job is to assist in the execution of the writer's intent. If the writer's intent is wrong, as it could conceivably be, then a good editor tries to refocus that intent, to cajole or tease or somehow seduce the writer into a better one. That's the tricky part. There are plenty of writers who complain that editors don't see what they are trying to do, don't give them a chance to do what they do best. These are usually not very successful writers. The editor won't let them have their way because they've failed to sweep the editor along. If the piece is strong enough, the question will never arise; if it's weak, the process of negotiating it into a strong piece requires flexibility on both sides.

I was a bad editor because I couldn't remove my own ego from the job, felt the need to impose my own sense of how the subject should be handled. I was far too heavy-handed. As a writer I'm hard to work with because I guard my writing from revision just as jealously as I guarded my prerogative as an editor to revise as I wished.

(Editing always hurts. It hurts to be improved, particularly when it is the product of your very best talent that is being improved. How could it not hurt, being improved?)

The editor's job as I see it is obviously different from that job as the editor sees it, and probably different from the job as management—the editor's boss—sees it. For me, it's a process of helping me get said what I'm trying to say, of catching me when I nod and straightening me up, keeping me on track.

The editor sees the job as cutting through the writer's idiocy and making him shut his blabbering mouth, making him push through to the real goal of the piece, which may not be what the writer thinks it is anyway. The publishing house seems to see the editor as someone who comes up with Big Ideas, or who corrals authors who come up with B.I.'s, and gets the author to produce those Big Ideas in the cheapest possible way, meanwhile generating blockbuster (but free) promotional ideas: Big Ideas that can be expressed in five words or less and that will immediately put the book on everyone's must-buy list, will make the dollars jump out of those (illiterate) readers' wallets. Big Ideas like One-Minute Low-Calorie Perfect Sex Anytime.

Good editing is one of those laborious invisible jobs, like housekeeping, that are apparent only when they aren't done, that can't by definition call attention to themselves, that make the world better but that reflect no direct credit on the people who poured the energy into them. I'm speaking of line editing here, the fine-grained detail work of getting writing into publishable shape.

The editor of my two previous books and this one is Amanda Vaill. When *Staying with It* was too long (and more than a little windy), she suggested a cut that started in the middle of one sentence and, two pages later, ended in the middle of another sentence, and worked perfectly. Dropped about four hundred words and improved the sentence on each end. One begins to trust an editor who does that kind of thing consistently.

• •

With regard to *Stone Work,* listen to the silence: no reviews, nothing happening. This month's Book-of-the-Month Club catalog should be out soon, and the book should be in it. I do keep hearing from people who heard my interview on *All Things Considered*. That show has a truly remarkable audience for books.

. .

Last night up popped an idea for what I think is a perfect next book for C. to write, the book she's been circling and circling but not quite able to see: *The Farm*. When she was growing up she spent summers—and escaped her large and chaotic family—on the farm of an aunt in southern Ontario. Every column that she's written in her "In the Country" series for *NEM* has grown out of her experience there; everything she knows and loves about gardening, animals, rural life, all come from that source. Most of her time there was in the company of her cousin Betsy, who has been saying overtly how much influence that farm had on their two lives, but C. couldn't quite break it open, hadn't yet seen that there was a book there waiting to be written. Now it pops clear.

Thinking about it later, I keep trying to get back to what was happening, what we were talking about, before that idea dropped—out of heaven, as it were. Can't get it back. What made it click into place?

I was reminded of that because this morning's work was so productive, I have such a nice rough draft in front of me, so roomy. I've been going through and going through it: three or four hours of the most delectable work, trying to get things said that I think worth saying. There's nothing I want more for C. than that she get a chance to enjoy that kind of writing time.

. .

Where this particular book idea came from: I happened once to meet Michael Crichton, the writer, film director, and medical doctor perhaps best known for *The Andromeda Strain.* When he published his nonfiction book *Travels,* I was struck by the clean control of the writing, and wrote to tell him so. I got back a nice note: "I must say the self-effacing or 'informal' style has its drawbacks, particularly since so often the reviews complain about the writing. There I am busting my back month after month scrubbing the sink of my prose and at the end of the line some clown says the book reads like it was 'thrown together.' I find it trying to be criticized for exactly the effect I tried so hard to achieve."

I loved the line about scrubbing the sink of his prose, and wrote back sympathetically. "In fact your letter has given me an idea for a little book," I said, "and I am starting a file. . . ."

. .

C. and I both have considerable capacity for meticulousness, but of course we're meticulous about different things. The object is to learn to be meticulous about things that count, I guess. Actually, C. has more capacity for it than I. She concentrates better. When you're concentrating on something, you're doing it as well as you can, as hard as you can, and I can imagine few greater pleasures than that.

Another great pleasure comes at those moments when you say, "Oh, I get it." This is closely aligned, in my mind, with the pleasure of having a rich, full slate of ideas ahead of you. Having a body of interesting ideas to play with is much more thrilling, pleasurable, and satisfying than, for instance, getting a good review in the *Times.*

That was why I got such an enormous kick out of the idea for *The Farm.* It's an idea that may very well slowly fade—C.

may not start to work on it for years, may never do it, may discard it for whatever reasons. But in the first flush of it, when more ideas are popping thick and fast, ideas about how to do it, that's the greatest pleasure in the writing game. That and rewriting are the two times when writing is truly fun. Honing a new idea is a much greater pleasure than publishing the finished work.

. .

I stop mowing to make a note about the dryness of the air, rare for July: so crisp that the view across the valley arranges itself into stacked vertical planes, as if there were nothing between one range of hills and the next, not even air.

Making notes about nature makes me pay better attention. I'm not much of a nature writer and never will be, lacking that feel for metaphor that seems to be required. I'd like to be one, though. The natural world is one of the things I'm happiest thinking about. Wouldn't it be nice to make a living writing only about the things it makes one happy to think about?

Ah, there's the noon whistle. It being July fifteenth, that makes it midday of midsummer's day, as I count things. Whoops, there I go, writing again.

. .

Borrowed to pay the property taxes, only because the second half of the advance for the *Log* is so perishingly slow in getting here. It set me raving about what we owe and are owed, about how all that's involved are pieces of paper that arrive in the wrong sequence. "Then it's all just a matter of tense," says C.

Politicians like to talk about how their unfortunate constit-

uents must live from paycheck to paycheck. This makes me
chuckle: we live from check to check and can't even predict
when the checks will come in. When it is necessary to establish
credit, I tell the banker that he should consider me something
of a farmer. I get an occasional cash crop, but there are a lot
of hailstorms and droughts in between. Bankers are not
amused by this analogy.

A few years ago, when the chaos of freelancing got too
much for me, I sought out a tax accountant. I took along some
old book contracts, to give the accountant some sense of how
book publishers do business. As he read over the contracts,
he kept muttering: "They can't do this. They can't do this.
Naw, come on, they can't *do* that. Can they?"

• •

The new Book-of-the-Month Club catalog does not feature
Stone Work, a momentary disappointment, but that means
they'll feature it in August, thereby extending the active life
of the book.

The mail also brought a dun from the town, fifty-odd dollars' interest and penalties on our unpaid taxes—which I'd
paid the day before. I notice that when *NEM* was struggling
with money problems, I was busy bitching about my own tiny
financial quandary. They were sweating a multimillion-dollar
problem, being nagged at by a lot more serious bill collectors
than I was. I am only neurotically insolvent; they were factually
insolvent. Freelancing does lead to a certain self-involvement.

• •

After *Stone Work*'s quiet week it was almost a disappointment to get another review, even though it's a good one: oh
hell, now I've got to make myself anxious about the book

again. I've never really believed anyone who claims not to read reviews, but I now understand that there's a valid rationale for that lofty position. I'd never be able to pull it off, but there's a good reason to try.

In an essay called "Waiting for the Book to Come Out," Phillip Lopate mentions how a hundred good reviews don't stir your mind as much as one carping line in an otherwise favorable review. Virginia Woolf says the same thing. I've been amazed at how much time I've wasted composing replies to critics who have been only slightly negative. The other day I had a long imaginary argument with a writer whose otherwise favorable review contained one line vaguely implying that I'd overlooked the difference between working with the brain and working with muscles. I thought I'd acknowledged that sufficiently, but obviously didn't hit it hard enough. It's pointless even to think about such things, but I manage to blow an amazing amount of time on them.

• •

The latest *NEM* contains Dick Todd's piece on the New York Yacht Club. I am thunderstruck, simply washed away by it as a piece of magazine writing: humiliated, as a writer, by how good he is. When the editor is so much better at writing than you are, you have the urge to gather all your loose notes into a wad and thrust it at him, saying, "Here, you do it. *You* make the damned thing work." Maybe that's why he once used a pseudonym.

• •

Noel Perrin reviewed *Stone Work* for *USA Today*, a sweetly favorable piece but with one perfectly accurate qualifier: "And if one were to make the comparison that the book begs for,

to Annie Dillard's *Pilgrim at Tinker Creek,* one would have to
say that in Jerome there's a little too much pilgrim and not
quite enough creek." That didn't hurt a bit, in fact gave me
a great laugh.

By a mildly amusing coincidence, there's a line in *Stone Work*
aimed directly at Perrin. He once wrote an encomium to his
chain saw, which struck me as misguided. So with him in mind
I included a comment about what a nasty machine I find the
chain saw to be. I dropped him a thank-you note mentioning
this. Also his piece, several years ago, about kissing his cat,
which I thought was wonderful.

. .

None of the reviews has suggested that *Stone Work* might
be about writing. That particular level of self-involvement
seems to have been successfully hidden.

. .

Shortly after *On Mountains* was published, I was asked to
talk to a high-school English class. The teacher drew me out
on the book's origins; I said that *Skiing* magazine had asked
me to write a piece about mountains, and, unable to find a
book that told me what I wanted to know, I wrote one myself.
I'd spent a lot of time in the mountains, knew mountains pretty
well, so I simply read twenty or so books, about various aspects
of the subject, and pulled out the information that fit my
project. A young man in the front row held up his hand: "If
the information was already in those other books, why bother
to write another one?" I sputtered, said something about the
possibility that the writing might add to or clarify the information, and changed the subject. And brooded about a better
answer all the way home.

. . . .

That night C. and I went out to dinner. A friend dropped by our table and mentioned that Walter Cronkite, on the TV in the bar, had just said that U.S. automakers had built seven million cars that year—and recalled seven and a half million. It was a nice little filler item, and the answer I wanted for that smart kid in the front row. Those two items didn't come over the wire together; some clever writer ran across one piece of information and wondered about the other, dug it up, and linked them in a way that made a telling comment about modern life. Linking two disparate pieces of information turned them into more than the sum of their parts. Something that could almost be called an idea was born.

Thinking about connection makes me remember what it was that caused the idea for a book about C.'s farm to happen. We were talking about childhood experiences, and C. kept referring to the farm. At some point it became clear that she had a great deal to say about it, that it had great emotional power for her, that it represented a substantive connection to her current world, and that that connection, properly illuminated by narrative, could be powerful for a reader—just as it was powerful for me as a listener. When that coin dropped, suddenly there was the idea. It is one of those ideas that have the power to extract material from underneath, that get you going, that generate good work.

The first thought that comes is that this would be fun to work on. The second thought is that maybe someone else would like to read about it. Perhaps I have those two thoughts in reverse order, but I believe that things that are truly engrossing to work on will end up better written than those aimed at grabbing a market. The writer will be clearer, more painstaking, more thorough in the writing of them. The subjects that are powerful to work on are also the ones that are going to pull the richest material up out of the unconscious. Then all that remains is to do the work of finding out, with the conscious mind, why these things are so rich, so powerful.

• •

Yesterday, visiting friends, we drove to Washington, Connecticut, a Disneyish village where life is posher than it has any right to be. We dropped by the local bookstore, one window of which was full of copies of *Talent,* a novel written by publishing mogul Howard Kaminsky and his wife, who were on hand signing books, filling the store with people. Dodging those proceedings, I looked for copies of *Stone Work* but couldn't find any. All the clerks were tied up by long lines at the cash registers—every bookstore should be so busy—but I wanted to inquire anyway: did they even have my book in stock?

Standing in line, however, I chanced to overhear a conversation between two couples, all four of whom worked in publishing. All I really caught was a snatch, to knowing laughter, about how these damned authors are always visiting bookstores and whining when there are no copies of their books on hand. I left without asking.

• •

Today brought the first of what I assume will be a series of nutball letters in response to *Stone Work:* some photos of a stone house under construction, copies of letters to and from the NIH Department of Health and Human Services proposing entirely new theories about "complementary biomolecules as potential autoantigens," and a copy of a letter from Freeman Dyson, telling the author that perhaps he shouldn't try to revise *all* the laws of mathematics and physics at once.

There was not one word anywhere about why this package was sent to me.

Nutball mail is only a mild distraction, reminding me that a certain firmness of purpose is required, which I am not always able to muster. There's a macho attitude, particularly on the staffs of periodicals, about cutting through distractions: about working effectively in the midst of chaos, producing against deadline. One is not put off by the buzzing gnats of modern life, one is a pro, able to buckle down and do the work in any situation. I've done that from time to time, sometimes even successfully, but I've never been deluded that I was producing better work that way.

How much better the work might be if we gave ourselves the right to do it without distractions, so that we could get at it, bear down on it. Of course then we'd have to learn *how* to get at it and bear down on it, a step that a lot of professional writers seem never to take. We keep the buzz around us, perhaps as a protection against ever having to find out how to drive the work into the corner, push it far enough.

When nonwriters talk to me about writing they always say they wouldn't have the discipline. Perhaps it isn't discipline, only interest. I go to my desk as quickly as I can get to it in the morning, simply because it is what I do, where I want to be. I can't get enough time at it. That isn't where the discipline comes in anyway. Where the discipline comes in is learning how to work when one gets there.

• •

It is finally beginning to sink in that this is something of a high point in my life, a period of great personal satisfaction and reward and, one would certainly hope, stability. I have this terrible hope that *Stone Work* will buy some time—and reduce the anxiety level in my daily life. I should know better than to expect the latter; even if it is a runaway success, all it will buy is time. If I'm going to reduce the anxiety level it'll have to be by other means—from somewhere beyond the reach of considerations like success and failure.

· ·

"The words used are the form of which the ideas are the content, and until the words have been found, the idea does not fully exist."—Northrop Frye.

· ·

Yesterday was the book signing at World Eye Bookshop in Greenfield: went okay, sold twenty or thirty books. Slightly discomfiting, all that standing around and chatting. I am struck once again by how destructive that kind of ego-pump is, how desperately distracting and uncentering that kind of public performance always turns out to be. Reminds me of running for class office in high school.

· ·

C. is off to Easton to pick blueberries, mostly as an excuse to spend a couple of days with her friend Ruth; I walk the loop on a hot, bright day, and stop to drink in the blue-green beauty of the woods, as rich as they ever get. We're still on the lush side of the summer. In a couple of weeks the subtle drying out will begin, the turning, the pulling-in. We haven't quite reached the crest of the hill, after which the slope goes down, over the next five months, into winter. This is peak: peak livableness, best temperature and air quality, exhilaratingly summery, before the dog days start hammering us down.

. . . .

• •

I've been reading *How to Be Happily Published,* which rubs my nose in an inescapable fact: the way to do it is to make oneself into a retailer, out there digging for every sale of every book. There are writers who fill a station wagon with cartons of their books and go on the road, peddling copies to everyone who'll hold still for them, speaking at small-town Kiwanis lunches, putting up card tables in malls. Publishers love these writers, I guess, but I didn't get into this line of work to become a retail salesman. Therefore I have to take the psychic lumps that result.

Which thought makes me realize I'm in a mild depression, on the downslope of reaction to the book. Nothing much more coming. Perhaps the *Times Book Review.* Three years of anticipation, paid off in three or four weeks, and then it's over. For the next book I must somehow distance myself from reviews and the reviewing process.

*Why not shoot yourself, actually, rather than finish one more
excellent manuscript on which to gag the world?*
                                        —Annie Dillard

A U G U S T

· · · · · · · · · · · · · · · · · ·

*T*he news this morning is that *The New York Times
Book Review* will review *Stone Work* on August 20.
The publisher just called to say it was scheduled
—and did I have a photo of myself with the dogs, or of Marty
and me? I did not—which, I suppose, postpones my son's first
appearance in the pages of the *Times Book Review.*

· ·

Funny book idea last night: *A Biography of My Wife.* I write
my version of C.'s life, then feed it to her for her corrections.
The title is a deliberate goof, withholding her name to indicate
that it's an ego trip on the part of the writer instead of a
serious treatment of the subject. C. doesn't seem particularly
amused by the idea.

The great good fortune of these conversations is that they
allow us to expose ideas as they occur—or fragments of ideas,
before they come together and grow coherent. It makes for
a dreamy and hopeful, if unrealistic, way of mulling over

future possibilities. None of them ever has to be tested by
putting word on paper unless and until it recurs and takes on
some kind of urgent life of its own.

• •

Barry Lopez, in "Mapping the Real Geography," says
that the U.S. was settled by means of a "false or
imposed" geography: "All local geographies, as they were
defined by hundreds of separate, independent native tradi-
tions, were denied in favor of an imported and unifying vision
of America's natural history. The country, the landscape itself,
was eventually defined according to the dictates of progress
like Manifest Destiny and laws like the Homestead Act, which
reflected a poor understanding of the physical lay of the
land."

His prescription for learning the geography of a place is,
simply enough, to question first the people who live on the
land and make daily use of it. That's a notion I was struggling
to understand, and get said, in the New Hampshire piece, but
I didn't take it far enough. It's a powerful prescription for
Place.

• •

C. has gone to a concert, I'm alone, enjoying a golden hot
humid evening, one of the finer evenings of the summer so
far, the world full of birdcalls and sunset light: the best time
of the day in the best time of the year in the best place we've
ever found to be. Wonderful deal.

• •

Willy sends a quote from a letter from his father to Ernest
Hemingway in September 1936:

156

· · · · · · · · · · · · · · · ·

The personal anguish in bringing out a book so far as I am concerned is simply unspeakable: the praise because I know it unearned is as bad as the blame which I think earned whether it was or not. If it weren't for that I could imagine that I wrote books for the same reason that they put scaffolding around a rotten peace [*sic*] of stone work—to support a self-confidence that won't stand by itself. But the actual repeated pain of the performance knocks that theory into a cocked hat. I'm left at the end of the row with nothing more philosophic than this—that I keep at it because nothing on earth makes me as happy as I am for about twenty minutes after I've finished a poem—and that I wouldn't be as happy as that (for some inexplicable reason) unless I knew that I would go ahead and smash the happiness by publishing the thing.

· ·

My waking image this morning was of Pawnee in her pen at dawn, leaping in place at the gate, wanting so badly to be out and free: that's how I want to get back into this manuscript. (What a bizarrely antiquated term "manuscript" is, implying a handwritten document. At the moment this "manuscript" consists of nothing but blips of light on a screen.)

It is a twitchy time. Part of my anxiety is probably the onset of seasonal depression. Yesterday I noticed the grass is picking up that subliminal red glow that signals the onset of foliage change. Gave me a characteristic wave of gloom.

Or my malaise could be physiological, a hormonal countersurge. For six weeks I've been living with large doses of adrenaline; now its chemical opposite must come flooding in. My adrenal gland's little tongue must be hanging out.

· ·

. . . .

The depression, I've decided, is definitely the seasonal one, to which I happen to have a mild sensitivity. Nothing else makes sense. This should be the happiest time of my writing life. We're entering the three most glorious months of the year, and I have a small success on my hands. For me to get depressed doesn't compute, at least from the standpoint of psychology. There's no possible psychological explanation for this mood swing, is there? What, guilt? Over good reviews? Naw. It is clearly the result of brain chemistry. It is hormonal, caused by nothing more than a change in the amount of daily sunlight: Seasonal Affective Disorder.

This is the black curse of the Freudian age. One can be seized by the chow dog of despair for no other reason than some chemical wash brought on by the change of the seasons, but Freudian folklore forces you to blame it on a character flaw. It must be caused by improper upbringing or improper methods of dealing with guilt or lack of expiation or whatever. I search frantically through all that gobbledygook for reasons for my gloom, when it is only that a change in the angle of the planet has caused a chemical change in my body.

If this were a primitive society—if I had a traditional culture—there would be temple images or some other symbolic representations of anger or depression, to give me a free pass. I wouldn't have to blame myself and my improper management of the world for making me sad, I could just be sad. I could lay it all at the feet of some figment of a roshi's vision.

At a cocktail party the other night, I overheard a shrink talking about sadness and our modern inability to deal with it. I leaped into the conversation, babbling, saying things— about sadness—that I had no idea were going to come out of my mouth. I was embarrassed afterward. Embarrassment is,

. . . .

after depression, the second most familiar feeling I associate
with autumn.

• •

A brilliant morning, and C. and I were out in it early,
determining to take a weekday off. We began the fall cleanup,
tilling the garden, getting the mowing done. While I was mowing I found myself getting miffed about payment for the *Log*,
and stopped to call Georges. Sure enough, the money had
arrived and they're issuing me a check today.

I asked about overseas sales; nothing has developed there.
I allowed as how we're getting enough good reviews that we
now should have something to sell. Yes, Georges said, they're
coming in nicely, and there was of course *The New Yorker*.
Gibbering noises on my end: *The New Yorker*? Yes, *The New
Yorker*.

Hadn't heard about that: surely it's one of the brief reviews?
Yes, said Georges sweetly, but it's a *long* brief review. This
news is an effective antidepressant.

• •

In three weeks C. goes to the writers' colony in the Adirondacks for a month's residence. She and I have arrived at
the decision, separately but simultaneously, to use this coming
separation—the first of this duration in twenty-five years—as
a kind of retreat, to find out what our true patterns are, how
our rhythms work.

We've been talking about the detailed knowledge we had
of our local surroundings—our turf—as children, and how
and when we lost that urgent need to explore. I think we
became socialized instead, getting our fulfillment from peers
rather than place. As children we were colonized first, then

· · · · · · · · · · · · · · · · ·

civilized. "I was an animal," C. says, "totally unsupervised." And how she hated to go indoors! She remembers approaching the house in the evening, after the day's play, seeing the light in the kitchen, and, despite her hunger, not wanting to go in—in part because there was such chaos in that household.

The last landscape that I knew with a child's intimacy was our small nonworking farm in New Braunfels, Texas. I was sixteen when we moved there, and knew at the time that I was already a couple of years too old to "play" on it in the way that would have revealed its true character to me. I was conscious of this, already wishing wistfully that I were a little younger. Just as I sometimes now ache to have ten-year-olds roaming with me over this land here.

I am ticked off at myself for not pushing the New Hampshire piece far enough to arrive at this idea. At one time I'd written a few lines into that piece—which were deleted for reasons of space—about how the locals know the location of every spring and rivulet. When I mentioned this to C., she told me of a search she'd made last month for the foundation of an abandoned hotel in the Adirondacks.

Unable to locate it on her own, she'd finally stopped at a local cabin and asked. The resident volunteered to show her the location. As they approached the site, he said, "There must be a new beaver dam in that brook. The water level's higher now." He knew the location of the lost foundation by the spring that served it, knew the local watershed at the micro-level. Just as our old friend Ion Whitcomb, a former highway department worker in Easton who is now in his eighties, knows every culvert in Grafton County.

· ·

Jud called to congratulate me on *The New Yorker* review, which I still haven't seen. He read it to me; brief but quite

favorable. Bruce called also, welcoming me to the pages of
that magazine, where his indescribable combination of satirical
art and writing appears from time to time. Getting even that
brief review there does have the feel of admission to a rather
more exclusive club than I'm used to.

• •

Dan Okrent is trying to talk Dick Todd into taking over
New England Monthly. Todd tells C. he's not going to do it. I
dropped him a note today threatening to come after him with
a stick if he leaves before the New Hampshire piece gets
edited.

• •

The check for the *Runner's Log* finally arrived; we'll be
solvent again for a little while.

I can't overstate the importance of the *Log* in my freelance
existence, or my gratitude for it. I inherited it from the late
James Fixx, whom I never met, who wrote it for its first seven
years. After his death the publisher passed it along to me. It
has not only helped smooth out our wildly oscillating financial
affairs, it has materially changed the way I work. To write the
Log required that I begin keeping a log for myself, which
eventually developed into a journal. I swore early on to keep
that journal private, but almost immediately broke that vow,
using it as a first run at what turned out to be *Stone Work.*
This book is the second that I've developed directly out of
that daily journal.

It won't be the last, because in current practice the journal
has become the first draft of everything I do. I go in and sit
down at the machine, and the place I start writing is my journal. It is an electronic notebook not only for first drafts but
for business affairs, weather details, correspondence, notes for

new projects as well as the slow accretion of text for the old ones. It is a rolling memo, which I get out of the way first thing in the morning, spending fifteen minutes or so at it, then figuring out what needs my attention first, setting the agenda for the day. It is not so much a repository of deep thoughts and personal secrets and private life as it is a kind of scratch pad for the day's work.

But everything in it is eventually coded to its true subject matter, and after I've gotten the immediate business of the day out of the way, I go through and, using the organizing power of electronic writing, flip the appropriate items into their own files. Moving the various ideas into new places serves a double purpose, because every time I move something out of the journal I review it, rethink where I might possibly use it, and, usually, polish it slightly; I see ways of touching it up, of changing the emphasis or reorganizing it for clarity. I begin to get a new look at what's underneath it.

"Each thought that is welcomed and recorded is a nest egg," said Thoreau in his own journal, "by the side of which more will be laid. Thoughts accidentally thrown together become a frame in which more may be developed and exhibited. Perhaps this is the main value of a habit of writing, of keeping a journal—that so we remember our best hours and stimulate ourselves. My thoughts are my company. They have a certain individuality and separate existence, aye, personality. Having by chance recorded a few disconnected thoughts and then brought them into juxtaposition, they suggest a whole new field in which it was possible to labor and to think. Thought begat thought."

· ·

Thinking about the *Place* book last night—as I was falling asleep—I decided quite firmly that it should be called, simply,

162

. . . .

Five Places. Subtitle to come. This morning, second thoughts: maybe *Intimate Landscapes: Five Places?* Anyway, the proposal will be fun to write, and perhaps I'll start it. A six-hundred-word precis of the Kiamichi piece, two hundred words each on the Comal, the Gulf Coast, and the West Texas town of Iraan, and then tack on the completed New Hampshire piece as a sample of "finished" work—although in book form that segment will be tripled in length.

. .

Spent the morning getting started on the *Places* proposal, which is beginning to work—and beginning to stir memories. That means I've had an absolutely engaging morning, writing not out of research or gathered information but out of my head. This is slightly frustrating, but only in the sense that writing is always frustrating. At least I have a clear sense of where I'm going and what I want to accomplish; I just have to find the way to say it, to get down the lines.

I break it off at noon with a great sense of optimism and confidence that this can be a fine book: an enjoyable book to read, a terrifically enjoyable book to write. This is as much fun as one gets as a writer.

. .

C. left early to run some errands—and by the way, to drop by the Broadside Bookshop to pick up next Sunday's *New York Times Book Review,* available on the Tuesday before the newspaper comes out. Which, I'd been told, would carry a review of *Stone Work.* I started to say, as she went out the door, "If I got the front page, call me from the store, okay?" But I didn't.

Stone Work didn't get the front page, didn't even get a full review. After entirely too much expectation on my part, it got only a paragraph in the "In Short" section, and, insult to injury, one of its worst reviews so far. "Occasionally bogs down," said the reviewer. "Might have been better with less."

Which lets the air out of that particular balloon. I'd let it get pumped too full anyway. Well, done and done—the last blip I expected on that book's radar screen. Its fate is now in the hands of the readers, the book buyers, and the booksellers. Nothing else for me to stew about until time to sell the paperback rights. No word yet about sales.

The New Yorker and the daily *Times* loved it, the *Times Book Review* did not. Go figure.

· ·

At lunch with Willy, expressing my recent doubts that *Places* will excite a publisher, I threw out the idea of *Biography of My Wife*. Willy thought it was a terrific idea, terrific title. So did I; wonder if I could possibly do it? I don't think so: it'd be a joke carried too far, a project entirely too fraught. I can see myself diving into it and finding, five thousand words deep, that it is impossible.

Still, it's on my mind. At breakfast this morning C. told me a story I hadn't heard before. Today happens to be the thirtieth anniversary of the sudden death of her father. She was fifteen; her mother had died, also suddenly, a year and a half before. The day her father died, the two of them had driven from Windsor to Toronto, where they saw a performance of *Brigadoon*. Afterward they visited adult friends of the family, who happened to have a daughter C.'s age.

She spent a long evening trying to talk to another teenager while the adults laughed and drank in another part of the house. Eventually it came time for the other young girl to go to bed, but C.'s father stayed on, and C. became angry at sitting alone at the late hour. Finally they went to a hotel, where they were given a single room, to C.'s further irritation. She was a young girl traveling with an older man; how did that look? She was of an age to be bashful about undressing in front of others. And he snored, a further irritation. Increasing, continuing anger at him. So they went to bed, and then her father began making gasping noises—at first C. thought he was only snoring—and died. The last thing he had said to C. was, "I'll try not to snore."

No wonder she's weird about my naps. She told me the story because she awoke this morning with the music from *Brigadoon* playing in her mind.

• •

Public-school teachers in Texas were required to do periodic graduate work, so, after my second year of teaching, I signed up for a summer course in business writing. I was the only enrollee, meeting with the professor in his office for fifteen minutes or so once a week. The requirements weren't stiff; I didn't actually have to write anything, but to get an A in the course I would have to sell a piece of writing somewhere.

I can't remember what we talked about, except that the prof once told me that when he needed spare cash, he'd go to the library, read the business pages of local newspapers, rewrite their stories, and submit them to the appropriate trade journals. He said he could make as much as five dollars an hour this way—not bad moonlight wages for an assistant professor in a jerkwater college in 1956.

I read the next day's *Dallas Morning News*, clipped an obituary for the late manager of a local pulp mill, found the address of a pulp-and-paper trade journal, rewrote the obit into a three-line item, and sent it off. Got back a check for two dollars, showed it to the prof, got my A. My first sale.

Five dollars an hour was heavenly spare-time pay for a high-school teacher, and during the next year I tried to duplicate my prof's success. I never sold another piece. One item did come back from a trade journal with a note saying that if I'd go interview local jewelry store owners about their window displays, write them up, and accompany them with good, sharp photos of those windows, they'd pay me a dime a word.

Not that trade journals aren't lifeboats for a lot of freelancers. When a writer I know made his first sale to *The New Yorker*, he was interviewed by then-editor William Shawn. Shawn asked him why he hadn't seen the writer's work before. "You must not have been reading *Auto Trim News* or *Modern Veterinary Practice*," the writer told him.

. .

To date *Stone Work* has shipped a measly eighty-three hundred copies, approximately the same figure reported back in May. At this point the publisher is waiting for the early shipments to sell out and reorders to come in. As the English music hall comedian says, wyte fer it, wyte fer it.

. .

The *Place* proposal so far:
Outside the confines of Oklahoma, the Kiamichis would scarcely be called mountains. They are the first real wrinkle in the landscape north of the Red River Valley, in the southeast corner of the state, making a scanty east–west range rising fifteen hundred feet above the surrounding flatlands. They are no more than foothills to the Ouachitas, which in turn are foothills to the Ozarks. But in Oklahoma City, in the depths of the Depression, we spoke often of the Kiamichi Mountains. They were the first destination I heard of, in a restless family,

that promised something like pleasure. The Indian name of
the place held no meaning for me, but "mountains" became
the first word I knew that connoted paradise.

My parents went there on fishing trips, to a dark little river
called the Mountain Fork, near the Arkansas border. Their
destination was always a small group of cabins—a "tourist
court," in thirties' parlance—owned by a Cherokee named
Coleman Ward. They would make the long drive through hot
summer nights, with my older brother, Jud, and me asleep in
the backseat, a canoe and fishing tackle roped to the top of
the car. By age four I had learned to rattle off in order the
last few towns—Hugo, Idabel, Broken Bow, Bethel—before
Coleman's place.

How or why the family first connected with the Wards is
lost in time. Jud, now in his sixties, says that when Dad's
drinking got out of hand, Mother would bundle us up and
strike off for the Kiamichis, which makes therapeutic sense.
On the other hand, it is firmly fixed in family legend that Dad
went there for the bass, as a dedicated fly-fisherman, and for
the cheap liquor, as a doomed alcoholic. Dry Oklahoma meant
bootlegger's prices; wet Arkansas was only eight miles away.

I don't remember the Kiamichis as mountains, don't recall
any heights. I remember only steep slopes along the river,
steep paths in the woods, no sense of altitude to the land at
all. Gradient simply made the woods more intricate, more
interesting. I do remember gray cliffs across the river from
Coleman's, and a waist-high waterfall, a ledge stretching across
the river with water spilling over it. I remember floating above
my father's naked back, his whiskers scratchy on my arms
around his neck, as he breaststroked out to an exposed rock
in the middle of the pool above the falls. (Decades later, when
I would swim with my own children, and then with my grand-

daughter, Addie, that memory always came back.) For me it wasn't mountains that made the Kiamichis attractive but the stretch of river across from the cabins—and the woods, to which I had unlimited access.

Coleman had acquired his little settlement when the reservations were broken up and their inhabitants reestablished on private land. The main cabin had once been a filling station and grocery store, but that enterprise was long abandoned, although gas pumps still stood outside. The shelves in what had become the Wards' living room no longer held general merchandise but canning jars, many containing venison, a staple in their diet. There was a small garden, a low barn and barn lot, chicken pens, a cow. Pigs and turkeys ranged free. Jud remembers following Coleman's horse-drawn plow, picking potatoes from the freshly turned furrow. The tourist court was really no more than a subsistence farm with extra cabins.

Coleman was a handsome small man with stark white hair and weathered face, fiercely proud of his Indianness. He wore a single feather twisted into his hair, so I wore one too for a while, an honorary Indian. He affected a kind of self-mocking patriarchy, handing down Indian wisdom and teasing everyone. I loved him insanely, saw him as an only slightly lesser God. Jud says he was a clown; he was that, too, the trickster version. His Indian name was Gray Fox, and the symbolism was perfect.

After my parents divorced I visited the Kiamichis one more time, on a camping trip with Jud and his Boy Scout patrol, chaperoned by Dad and our new stepmother, Evelyn. Dad's role was de facto Scout leader, but he sliced open his hand in a fishing accident and began drinking again—or began drinking again and then cut his hand—and withdrew to the cabins, leaving the Scouts virtually on their own. It was a summer camp run by the kids, a paradise, albeit with ticks and poison ivy. Jud and his accomplices were in their midteens, I was not quite ten.

I was in heaven. Coleman taught us a little woodcraft, but a grandson named Tecumseh—called "Teacup"—taught me more. When I wasn't camping and swimming with the Scouts, I played in the woods behind the cabins with Teacup, a year or so older than I. Sometimes we were joined by his sister, Felicia—"Witchie"—who was about my age and with whom for at least ten days I fancied myself in love. Teacup and Witchie were exotics, clearly tougher, faster, and stronger than any kids I'd ever known. They ran through brambles barefoot, ignored the searing summer heat, ate anything, demonstrating precisely the brand of Indianness that movies and books had prepared me to expect. I was in awe.

We roamed the woods, harassed the farm animals, conducted various more or less scatological experiments. We played Indians against imaginary Cowboys (I refused the role of enemy). They taught me to chew "rabbit tobacco," a nondescript local weed that was perfectly tasteless but produced copious amounts of spit, a valuable resource for nine- and ten-year-olds. They bullied me a little, challenging me to match their toughness. As the paleface I accepted bullying as my appropriate fate.

I was free to run with them all day, encountering adult supervision only at meals and bedtime. Each night I had to undergo a strip search for ticks. By that hour Dad was usually unconscious, so the responsibility devolved to Evelyn. I was required to take off all my clothes and stand, squirming, beside a kerosene lantern, while she inspected my every mortified, hairless inch. When she found a tick she would pluck it gently, and scrape it off her fingernail into the chimney of the lamp, where it would incinerate with a momentary tiny flare in the dark cabin. What quivering humiliation—and titillation—there was in that, standing naked before sweet Evelyn, Dad's sainted second wife. (Mother, I knew, would no longer put up with him; Evelyn would.)

That summer's climax came with a daylong community hunt. Coleman's four adult sons, various other male relatives and friends, and Teacup joined in; the Scout patrol and I were invited along. There was an almost military organization to the day. The group would split up and go off in different directions, meeting hours later at mysterious specified places in the woods. Adult conferences were held about what to do next. We spent much of the morning "noodling"—grappling fish by hand from under logs and mudbanks in the sloughs and ponds. That was as frightening a task as I've ever attempted, there being snakes and turtles as well as sharp-finned catfish under there. An occasional live thing brushed my fingertips, but, shirking duty, I caught nothing.

One communal rifle and one barebacked horse were available; from time to time an adult would take both and disappear, hunting deer. Noodling and summer deer hunting were both illegal, of course, as was virtually everything else we did in the woods that day, but one of Coleman's participating sons was the local game warden. Otherwise, Coleman explained, life in the woods was too complicated. How were you going to live if you couldn't take game? Better to install a relative in the office.

My assigned role was to stick with Jud and Coleman, and stay out of trouble; Teacup was allowed to do serious hunting with the men, and I was jealous of that. After the noodling, I didn't see him again until late afternoon. While Coleman had taken the Scouts and me on a long hike elsewhere—

probably to drive deer toward the waiting rifle—Teacup had joined an uncle who was fishing a stock tank with rod and reel. The uncle hooked a good-sized bass, but it snapped the line and took his plug. Couldn't let fish *and* plug get away, so Teacup waded in to grapple the fish to land.

Just as we walked up to the pond, I saw Teacup stand upright in waist-deep water, one arm raised high, his forearm level over his head. A three-pound bass, flapping wildly, dangled from his arm. One of the plug's fishhooks was embedded in the mouth of the bass, another in the meat above his wrist. He waded calmly over to shore, where his uncle removed the fish but not the hook. Discussion followed. It wasn't clear whether the hook had snagged a tendon. If not, it could simply be cut out; if a tendon was involved, the hook would have to be pushed on through the flesh to emerge at a second point. Then the barb could be clipped off and the hook backed out from under the tendon. Finally someone showed up with the horse, which had functioned as a kind of circulating taxi throughout the day, and Teacup was sent home on it. The women would solve the problem; we men would go on hunting. I suppose we did; I don't remember much else about the day. Teacup admitted that it hurt, but his lip never trembled. I wish I could say the same for myself.

That was my last trip to the Kiamichis. Dad died a few years later, and the Kiamichi Mountains were, for our family, finished: he had been the force that got us there. But by then they had lodged in my underconscious as Ur-mountains, the source of everything wild, my connection to the natural world for the rest of my life.

The current topographical map shows the Mountain Fork to be dammed now, a man-made recreational lake backing up to within a few miles of Coleman's little settlement. What for us was an entirely untamed and unspoiled corner of the state is now surely overrun with recreational vehicles and bass boats. Black dots on the map, however, indicate Coleman's old location. I want to go see what still stands, or what it has become. Teacup—formally Judson Tecumseh Ward, named after my brother—should be close to sixty now. I intend to see if I can find him, and Witchie. I want to see those mountains as an adult, and get at the lay of that land. I want to find that rock above the falls, and swim out to it.

· ·

End of Kiamichis; that's eighteen hundred words, three times longer than I wanted it to be, but I don't think I'll cut it. It's not exactly loose. I'm ready to start into the rest of the proposal. The other four places I have in mind:

Bayou Country: during World War II, I lived in the small, totally artificial town of Old Ocean, hastily thrown up to house workers for a new aviation-gasoline refinery in the sweltering coastal plain of Texas. Air-conditioning was not yet available; sixty inches of annual rainfall supported a prodigious mosquito population. Old Ocean was populated by families imported for the war effort, and was a raw and lawless place. School was in nearby Sweeny, a sleepy small town where most of the boys and some of the girls chewed tobacco, and came to school barefoot much of the year. The Old Ocean–Sweeny region has now become one of the petrochemical capitals of the world, a nightmarish environmental hell. It wasn't paradise when I lived there, but it supported a level of outdoor adventure entirely satisfactory for our pubescent purposes.

The Comal: a sparkling little gem of a river, only seven miles long, originating in clear-water springs that bubble up below the limestone cliffs of the Balcones Escarpment in Lyndon

Johnson's Central Texas. The town within which the Comal lies, New Braunfels, was established by a German prince in the mid-nineteenth century, and settled almost entirely by German immigrants; when I entered its high school in 1948, most of my schoolmates had learned English in the first grade. The Comal remains at a comfortable temperature year-round, and I spent every available moment in it, swimming its every inch. The river is the story.

West of the Pecos: the tiny oil-patch town of Iraan, in the rimrock country of far West Texas, on the banks of the Pecos River. This is the lower edge of the *Llano Estacado,* or Staked Plains, the eastern lobe of the great American desert, with five inches of annual rainfall, open-pit oil wells, Indian caves, and wild javelinas; it is former buffalo range now spotted with fifty-thousand-acre sheep ranches. I taught school there in the late fifties. It is a geography—and population—at contrast with what most of us understand the United States to be.

The Geography of Dreams: a small mountain valley in New Hampshire, about which I've written for *New England Monthly.* I'll include the magazine article to show approach and treatment; for the book I'll expand the piece, putting in more people, telling the whole tale.

Each of these places provides, in addition to a rich stew of good stories, a specific and very different landscape and physical geography. Each opens the possibility of sharply contrasting memories against the present tense; my own experience with each supplies a gap of time against which to measure change. The approach in every case will be to get down the physical geography—and some of the history—of what Barry Lopez calls intimate landscapes.

In part this will be a book about pre-electronic life in the United States, about the places people lived when we weren't connected instantaneously to everyplace else in the world. It's a book about how we are rooted in the natural world, rooted in ways that we don't know, never think about: rooted in physical geography; informed—and formed—by the geography of place. *Five Places* will be a book about how place shapes lives.

• •

Um, a little rhetorical, that. Well. I'll let it sit for a few days, in hopes it will sprout new ideas.

• •

It'll be more of a memoir than I want to admit. One point—about place—is that my family did happen to move around a great deal. Jud once counted twelve schools he'd attended by the sixth grade, a figure my mother hotly denied until he named them for her. I think I want to write it because any place we lighted long enough to acquire anything like a close acquaintance with the landscape became special to us.

Pause to think about how to make *Place* more attractive to a publisher—when I already know what the book is going to be. What a pitiful commentary: here I am working out Machiavellian strategies for the exposure of the idea, instead of developing the idea itself.

Before starting on the proposal proper, I bounced a snapshot description of it to Georges Borchardt, expressing concern about its regionalism. "I don't think you need worry about the regional appeal problem," he replied. "After all, Bruce Chatwin's *In Patagonia* did sell copies outside of Patagonia. . . ."

I also tried the idea on Amanda Vaill, whose response was more complex. I should think of making the book only about New England, or only about the Southwest, she suggested.

"Doing that makes the book about the *subject;* writing about how the Southwest and New England have shaped you makes it about *you* . . . and I think The Reader is going to feel more attracted to a book with a more external subject. I also think that overtly focusing the book on an external subject allows you to make the point about [your personal] connectedness by teasing it out of the material. It makes the connection part of the payoff, rather than the handle, as we say in sales. And something as ephemeral as 'connection' doesn't give you the strongest handle."

Good point. A handle is what we lack here, folks. But it'll come, it'll come.

. .

It is the golden end of August—the angle of the light changing, the woods almost bugless, with cool bright clear sharp mornings—and C. and I are preparing, with not a little trepidation, for her departure. Agent Don Congdon calls to say he's gotten an offer for C.'s book, too low but he thinks he can bump it up a bit. If he succeeds, she'll probably take it. All of this falls in place perfectly for her departure for the Adirondacks: she goes off with a book contract in her knapsack.

We talked at some length about doing the book for what will still be insufficient money, the arguments for which are complex, and subtle. It has a lot to do with reduction of pressure on a first book. She's willing to underwrite a bit of it herself, to get a solid book behind her, get her name established. Depressurizes her first long project. The editor and agent aren't going to be terribly interested, but also are not going to be terribly pushy, which will free her up to do what she wants with it.

I of course couldn't resist mentioning that my first real book, *The Death of the Automobile,* brought the munificent advance, in 1970, of fifteen hundred dollars. I wrote it to a hard outline, absolutely terrified of violating that outline in any way: I had no idea where the book might go if I stepped out of those boundaries.

• •

C. leaves tomorrow; I make a rush trip into town for charcoal about 7:00 p.m., on a glorious, wild, roaring, windy evening, low sun and crashing tree limbs, just beautiful. As I return I invent a book to be entitled *Thirty Days Without C.:* a meticulous observation of the crazed and no doubt depressed time that I am in for. I think I am trying to give myself permission to do nothing but write in my journal for thirty days.

One wants simply to sit on a bank and throw stones.
                              —Virginia Woolf

                  S E P T E M B E R
• • • • • • • • • • • • • • • • •

*A*t ten-thirty C. left for the Adirondacks for a month. I find myself . . . stunned. I went upstairs and plunged into work, pushed the manuscript ahead for a page or two, quit for lunch and a walk. It's a curious, flat, still, gray day, rather airless: mystifying, a day that isn't here. Waves of sadness. I hope she's busy enough to be escaping this.

                         • •

Labor Day softball at a friend's over in Worthington, not too bad a time. Todds and Okrents were there, and various Worthington locals; I schmoozed and had a couple of beers. Home again, after a self-indulgent dinner, I sat on the deck at sunset watching little dots of golden cumulus clouds drive by. Sat there off in my head, thinking of seventeen other things while on the north wind these little spots of glory paraded by me one by one, saying here we are, look at this. And me unable, in my internal scurrying, to take them in. Mr. Jerome, said

                                                            177

Christopher Lehmann-Haupt, cannot get out of his head. Exactly. And writing—turning what one thinks into sentences—may be the worst possible thing to do if one can't get out of one's head.

• •

Playing softball for the first time in a couple of decades was very strange, calling on skills I once had but hadn't practiced in years, and was not at all sure I could still perform—even catching the ball, or throwing it, or, certainly, hitting it. When the ball came my way, all this sudden responsibility came showering down on me; I was supposed to do something reasonably athletic about it, and hadn't done any of those things in twenty years. There was an underlying panic: if I tried too hard I was probably going to injure myself, but I was unable *not* to try hard, just to fulfill the social contract. It was very complicated. Underneath it there was this middle-aged voice saying slow down, slow down, relax, take your time, but that voice had no effect at all. Anyway, I survived intact.

• •

Noon on Sunday, our twenty-third wedding anniversary: I am sitting in the sun at the top of the hill being astounded at how beautiful everything is. Maybe if I play my cards right I can spend today doing that. And stop writing.

This is my anniversary present from C.: to be forced to sit at the top of the hill and notice things. Forced to climb out of the Sunday *New York Times* and look at the world. Of course I'm also being forced to listen to my neighbor's chain saw. It is one of those occasions when I find myself trying to gobble up the details with my eyes, knowing it is a time I'll want to remember. Gobbling up details with the eyes is planning for

the future, which means losing the present, doesn't it? Strange
gift: I feel much closer to C. on this anniversary than any
other, ever, because in her absence I have no choice but to
think, almost exclusively, of her.

• •

Places proposal: I read *For Whom the Bell Tolls* when I was
sixteen, and like most other adolescent males fell in love with
Hemingway. I think it was the opening of the book that did
it, Jordan lying on the forest floor, smelling the pines. It placed
me not in the Pyrenees but in the Kiamichis.

The *Places* proposal is nearly done, pushed along nicely this
morning, needing only fine-tuning. I'm struggling with the
title now: *Five Places: Intimate Landscapes*, I think. *Five Hard
Places* is still in the running. *Intimate Geographies?*

When the New Hampshire piece goes into the book, I want
to change its tone. I want to make the benevolence and beauty
of the place shine through its hard nature. I'll speak only in
the most positive terms about all of these places, of their beauty
and charm and all that (using none of those words). And then,
without comment, acknowledge that there are indeed ticks
and poison ivy and blasted winters and searing summers. The
sometimes horrible, scouring weather. I want to get in some
of the human generosity with which e.e. cummings described
his captors in *The Enormous Room*. I want to get and keep that
cummings-ish, Whitmanesque, accepting mode firmly in mind
when I write.

• •

In C.'s absence I find myself doing things exactly as when
we're both here, not to interrupt the normal flow. I wash up
carefully after each meal, put the dishes back in exactly the

179

same place at the same time. My grasp on the household feels very tenuous; if anything gets a sixteenth of an inch out of line, I panic and smash it back into place with a hammer.

• •

After a couple of days of avoiding my desk, I found myself last night compulsively writing, trying lines, composing sentences. ("How I should like," said Virginia Woolf, in the middle of a wearying motor trip on the continent, ". . . to write a sentence again! How delightful to feel it form and curve under my fingers!") The Lehmann-Haupt line about getting out of my head keeps reverberating; yes, and my mantra is Stop Writing. Without C. here, I talk to the tape recorder instead. Maybe that's why she signed up for a month away.

• •

No *Stone Work* news: my six weeks seems to be up. The operation was a success but the patient died. Perhaps the patient is still on the respirator.

• •

The woods are dark and cool, the spots of sunlight blinding. I stop to look hard at a patch of sunlight and marvel at the way all those insects have gathered in that particular spot of sun. Then I realize that it isn't that insects have gathered there, but that the patch of sunlight makes visible the insects already there, always, in summer, there.

I take the dogs with me into the pasture above the house; they wander around smelling things, I sit on the rock ledge beneath the large maple in the golden September sun, enjoying the details: fumbling bees among the wildflowers, a sweet little breeze out of the northwest, puffy cumulus clouds in a deep blue sky. The sunlit green of the mowed field below me is so vivid in the late afternoon that shadows on it look blue-black. It's a quality of light I've never seen captured on film, and I have a momentary urge to go call Hans and ask if he's gone outside this afternoon to look at the light.

Collecting details, I notice, is what I do when I'm not sure what I should be looking for—a dike, I suppose, against the panic of an unoccupied mind. It is not an entirely satisfactory activity. In grade school the teacher was forever pointing out the descriptive passages, claiming they were beautiful. We would have preferred to get on with the story, never mind that boring crap about purple clouds and silver moonlight. Descriptive writing was just another one of those adult swindles. Now, suspended between my own narratives, I catch myself working the same old con.

Sitting under a tree and absorbing details isn't exactly writing, but seems to spring from the same scrambling panic. In one of Thomas Merton's journals he quotes the Russian writer Rozanov: "Gogol looked *attentively* at Christ, and threw away his pen and died."

What is excruciating about this separation is that it is so clearly the best thing C. could possibly be doing, and the best thing I could possibly be doing. It's perfect, there's no way I can rail against the injustice of it. No way I can bitch and whine and call it unfair: can't get at it.

. .

This too is part of the writer's life: I just discovered that (a) *Stone Work* has still shipped only eighty-five hundred copies, and (b) there are no paperback rights to be sold. Or I already sold them, same difference. Out of idiocy, or naïveté, I overlooked this, or forgot about it, at the time I signed the contract (four years ago last month). I'm sure Georges told me, but I wasn't listening. The publisher held on to the paperback rights and will issue the book in that form in approximately a year. I'll then get seven and a half percent of the publication price of paperback copies sold. Period. If, that is, the advance has been earned back. Of course I was dreaming of a sizable paperback sale to bail us out of our continuing financial hole.

. .

The weather continues uncannily brilliant. Seventy-five yards into the woods I find myself wrapped in velvet: the air is perfectly cool and sweet and moist, there are a zillion insects around but none around me, the light is golden, the woods are softening toward their coming collapse. It's heaven in here. And I feel compelled again to write it down.

The beauty of the woods is eerie, keeps snatching at my attention, snatching me back, making me feel as if I'm seeing them for the first time. C. has been urging me for years to go off and spend some significant time alone. Go visit a monastery or something. I wouldn't do it, so she did. Another gift.

Biography of My Wife: For several years now I've wanted to write a biography, but haven't found a subject who motivated me to make the effort. Then it occurred to me: why not write a biography of someone to whom I have very good access? This need not be a famous person. In the biography of a famous person, the subject pulls the book; why not write a biography for the form itself? Why not try to find the differences between the way a biography would be written if pulled along by the subject and the way a biography would be written if its only responsibility were to do the most complete portrait possible of the subject?

There I go, writing again. A joke proposal.

· · · · · · · · · · · · · · · · ·

· ·

I sit down on a rock in the woods, and the dogs come swirling around, dismantling the stillness. I suppose I bring the dogs along in order not to be alone. Alone at my machine, I keep writing in order not to be alone. I will not be alone in the same way I will not stop writing; I keep moving to avoid being alone. My frenetic activity, my sense of urgency, is to keep myself in motion, so I won't have to acknowledge aloneness.

This is getting a little crazy. *Zen and the Art of Motorcycle Maintenance* and *Pilgrim at Tinker Creek* come to mind. Both depict the internal lives of slightly disturbed individuals—and were quite successful books. Maybe people like to read about crazed individuals. Maybe it gives readers permission to admit a little of their own craziness.

· ·

Just finished the loop, making copious notes the whole way, but somehow never actually got the tape recorder turned on. Screwed up with the control buttons. Just as well.

· ·

The ninth beautiful day in a row but gradually deteriorating, the nights growing warmer, the days hotter. Had to quit at eleven to go run errands in town: how hard it is to get anything done, how logistics distract, how this great work period I anticipated is being fiddled away in household management. How much of the logistical needs of this operation are taken care of by C. Maybe I'll be better at it next week.

Letter from her this morning glowing with happiness, reveling in the whole experience.

183

• •

This morning at the post office Ruth Craft, who grew up on the place where we live now, stopped me to tell me how much she was enjoying *Stone Work*. "I nearly cried when I read that the sugarhouse had come down," she said. "I remember my dad building it in 1938 or 1939." She said she wants to come up and walk around the place with me sometime. I'd love to have her do that.

We've known Ruth since we moved here ten years ago, but I always felt a veil between us. Maybe *Stone Work* satisfies her that we properly appreciate her former home. This piece of land went through other owners—and the original house was replaced with a new one—before we bought it, but I've also imagined an undercurrent of resentment from our immediate predecessors on the place. It's uncomfortable. The property was on the market because of a family reversal, as with a great deal of real estate. (C. reads mansion ads in the Sunday *Times*, the multimillion-dollar estates that have come on the block. She always wonders, she says, what went wrong in those expensive lives.) We purchased their home, took it from them, even if by doing so we helped them solve a problem.

When I meet a stranger, as at a cocktail party, I usually ask where "home" is. I've been doing it for years. The answer is usually at least partially defensive. I wonder what home is, in America. What percentage of the people who work in the media, politics, government, the academies are living within a hundred miles—or five hundred miles—of the town where they graduated from high school? The formation of opinion in this country must be almost entirely in the hands of people who have left home—for whatever reasons, with whatever effect it had on their values. I don't even know if I know anyone who lives where he or she grew up, except for a few old-timers in small New England villages.

Maybe I've been disguising from myself the true intent of *Places*. What the book is about is place; why not call it that? Why not let that be the true subject? Not a scholarly discussion but a familiar one—a long familiar essay on the subject of place.

I remember driving through Bennington, Vermont, years ago on a September afternoon, seeing the kids dawdling home from school, and feeling almost through my pores how much they must want to get out of that idyllic small-town America —when C. and I wanted nothing more at the time than to immerse ourselves more deeply in it. Americans devote a great deal of attention and energy to doing what we want to do and having what we want to have, leaving almost to happenstance the question of where we want to be. Yet that surely has as much to do with happiness as the achievement of those other two goals.

When we're growing up, where we want to be is only some-place else, somewhere other than where we are. *Place* needs an extended essay on shaking the dust of that burg—whatever burg it is—off our heels.

The book should be in large measure about the tension between leaving the land and staying on it, between those who leave and those who stay, and the different world views that result.

I've been dancing around this subject. I've even been re-ferring to the project as "Place," or "Places," but I haven't yet summoned the boldness to go ahead and pitch the book as what it certainly intends to be: a study of the meaning of place. That's too big and too philosophical an idea; I'm afraid of pitching it in a few lines in a book proposal, where I don't have room to develop it properly.

• •

Finally managed to write to C. She's having a great time, I'm having a . . . powerful one. Hers is all new, full of intriguing experience; I'm having exactly the life I want to have here, but without her presence it is insufficient, and I am not creative enough to come up with a life that is sufficient in these circumstances. I can't think what is lacking.

She was worried that I'd be depressed over the business of paperback rights. I told her not to worry, that it was just one more of those delusions that keep me from getting realistic about my own product. I need to find a little more attractive book project to do next, but the Big Idea refuses to come. Also, she'd suggested that we skip the Caribbean vacation next year, for reasons of time as well as money; I'd already come to the same conclusion. Better to stick close and get some work done. I'm actually looking forward to a real winter, some of it, perhaps, in the Adirondacks.

• •

Continuing silence re *Stone Work,* despite the reviews. For some reason this has me remembering a magazine piece I once wrote entitled "The Age of Enlitenment," about how diets simply do not work. It was published as my regular monthly column in *Outside* magazine, and I got paid whatever they were paying me for that at the time. Then it was picked up by another magazine, and another, and continued to sell for a couple of years, usually at something like a hundred or two hundred dollars a pop. It hardly made me rich, but it tripped some lever in the editorial imagination, and was by

· · · · · · · · · · · · · · · · · ·

far the most popular magazine piece I ever wrote. Obviously, I should just write a goddamned diet book or some other public swindle and climb out of this economic hole we're in.

There is a wonderful book lodged in the back of my mind, one that I've been wanting to write for years, about the use of dogs in polar exploration. The reason Amundsen made it to the South Pole and Scott did not was that Amundsen used dogs and Scott used men: man-hauling, they called it, dragging their own sleds. Vilhjalmur Stefansson was a famous exception among explorers because he treated his dogs well. There are subtle mentions, here and there in the literature of polar exploration, of how important the dogs were psychologically, as companions, even as heroic inspiration, to the explorers.

On the other hand, Amundsen used many dogs while the sleds were heavily laden, but when the sleds got lighter he reduced their number (and saved additional food and weight) by killing the extra dogs and feeding their carcasses to the dogs that remained. Then—the logical next step—he and his crew killed and ate the remaining dogs themselves, thereby maintaining the necessary strength to finish their task.

I would like to dig into the subject of dog training (a rich literature), and into polar exploration (a richer one). Go to Norway and dig documentation out of the libraries. Immerse myself completely, then write the story from the dogs' point of view. Dogs work so well with us because they are pack animals and accept human beings as pack leaders, Alpha males: gods. On a polar exploration, they are working for their gods; their gods eventually murder them, feed them to each other, eat them themselves.

This is a perfect example of a completely absorbing book to write, one that would take about five years of extremely hard work, and would draw an advance from almost any publisher of, oh, ten thousand dollars.

. .

Home from three days in the Adirondacks with C., a remarkable vacation: three days of intense attention to things as they are. Didn't make a note, didn't have a note to make. See other book.

I returned to relieve the house sitter of five rather frantic animals. When I opened the car door Pawnee jumped in and wouldn't get out—by God I wasn't leaving again without her. For the next twenty-four hours I basically had three cats in my lap and two dogs at my feet. The cats went through four cans of food overnight.

. .

"See other book": readers of *Great Heart* will recognize the reference. That wonderful book tells the story of three early-twentieth-century canoe explorations of Labrador. The first, a three-man attempt, was a disaster, ending in the death by starvation of the leader and a narrow escape for the other white man and the native guide. The leader's widow determined to finish her husband's work with a new expedition, and hired the same native guide to help her. The other survivor mounted a competing expedition. Both of these later expeditions were ultimately successful.

The widow's adventure gains considerable poignance when the native guide, a good-hearted simple soul, falls quietly in love with her, and begins to harbor deluded notions that their postexpeditionary fates might be intertwined. His journal survived the expedition, but some kind of Victorian propriety compelled him to consign his emotional life to another, secret place. When his longings overcame his reticence, he would write in his journal "See other book." That other book, whatever it had to say, remains private to this day.

. .

On the Friday before I left for the Adirondacks, C. got another, better offer for her book. She told Congdon she'd think about it. Then, she said, not only did she not feel any of the elation that she'd expected at finally selling her book, by the time she got back to her room, she was positively depressed.

On Sunday, however, she got two more offers. One was from Ed Burlingame at Harper & Row, who has his own colophon and knows and loves the Adirondacks. She's probably going to accept it. For a proposal that was generated in January, it has been a tedious process, but she's in business, a practicing book writer, contract virtually in hand. I couldn't be happier.

The startling part of this saga has been agent Don Congdon, who just kept trolling away, despite early turndowns and offers that were positively insulting. It has been a remarkable performance by an agent for a new client who has never written a book. I had the urge this morning to write him, congratulating and thanking him for his efforts—but I didn't, having learned by now (I hope) not to overparticipate in one's spouse's endeavors.

. .

Last night I gave a reading at the local library. Sharing the bill were Mary Priscilla Howes and Linwood Lesure, two elderly locals who have written sprightly memoirs—and, in Mary Priscilla's case, surprisingly good poetry—about life in our little town of Ashfield in former times. Their part of the evening was charming; I have no idea how mine went, but rather enjoyed doing it once I got started. I had a little initial trouble with my voice, from being too enamored of my own prose.

• •

Okay, how do I write a book about Place? Witold Ryb-czynski has done a fine job with a similarly basic concept, in *Home: A Short History of an Idea*. His book is very different from what I have in mind, but demonstrates that a popular book can be done on an utterly simple idea.

It's fairly clear that I can't do it with a memoir about five places. C. says perhaps the progression should be geology, geography, history, and social history: move up through time from the eternal, or seemingly eternal, to the ephemeral. Maybe the entry point is a series of essays—geology, or the various aspects of physical geography, Jones's attitude-and-altitude, weather, climate, soils, flora and fauna. I don't want to do a sociological look at our national restlessness—see Jud's twelve schools—unless I can do it anecdotally.

I'll likely still use the five place essays, but pull them down in length to four or five thousand words, use them as end-papers between major sections of the book that more formally examine the questions of place. I don't want to get into one of those pseudoscientific looks at the effects of physical geography on lives. People's eyes glaze over at the words "physical geography." I want to find some way to pose the question in a very immediate way.

Maybe the critical question has to do not with those who've left the land and those who haven't, but with those who have left the land and have no impulse to get back to it, as compared with those for whom getting back to it is a driving force.

Place is the handle Amanda Vaill is looking for, as well as the title. That's the bigger idea; it solves the question of combining New England and the Southwest. The idea of place, the power of place, the meaning of place. There's a book there. I haven't got it yet but it's there. I'll let it sit again.

. .

One of the amusing things C. and I talked about over our recent weekend was the difficulty we found in writing letters to each other: in finding the honest voice, shorn of all ornamentation, all writerliness, that would be suitable, after twenty-five years of cohabitation. What a strange comment that is about writing, and about voice: that it should be more difficult to speak directly to the person with whom one is most intimate than it is to speak to unknown multitudes of readers out there. (Well, dozens anyway.) But it is precisely that shearing away of writerly tricks—deceptions and poses and personalities and identities and self-conceptions—that I want as a writer to pursue most assiduously.

. .

Last evening Hurricane Hugo knocked out the power, leaving me sitting in the dark; God having turned off the TV, and my eyes being too weak for reading by candlelight, there wasn't anything else to do with my mind but let it spin out book proposals. Or pursue ideas and ways to write about them, which kept turning into book proposals.

One of them seems to be seriously engaging my attention. The idea, strangely enough, grew directly out of grooming the dogs—bathing them, brushing them out, clipping the accumulated burrs out of their coats. I was struck by how eager they were for the contact, how needy. I'd thought I was going to spend this month alone, but with two dogs and three cats —and only one person here to dispense attention—it is more like going to live on a commune for a month.

The book idea, still quite loose and unformed, would be a study of how we understand, or try to understand, animals. How man works with animals. I've been looking for a way to write about animal behavior for years now. I once proposed to raise and train a dog, and write a book documenting the process: the dog would obviously teach me to train animals at the same time I was teaching it to coexist with people. Two publishers made offers, neither large enough to support the book. Maybe the way for me to approach the subject is to select a single aspect of animal behavior: our contact with them, their contact with us.

It would require that I study the training of animals, the scientific observation of animals, the management of animals. There are all sorts of interesting things to investigate: research showing changes in blood pressure and blood chemistry from touching pets (geriatrics specialists are instigating petting zoos for rest homes); the chimpanzee-gorilla language question, the tons of dolphin research, the recording of whale sounds; the elaborate and careful observation by Goodall and ilk; Bernd Heinrich (a personal hero of mine), who has worked with bumblebees, owls, and has just published a book about ravens. Ted Grand, a functional anatomist at the Smithsonian's National Zoo, once volunteered to put me in touch with the best animal person for any species I wanted; that lead alone makes me eager to do such a book.

I suppose it'd be a sort of ultimate New Age, touchy-feely environmental book. That doesn't mean it's not a decent and

192

serious one to write. It certainly opens up a roomful of beautiful things to study and think about. In the Adirondacks we walked up on some semitame deer, and I caught myself making chirping noises, trying to call them closer. Reminded me of Hoagland's wonderful essay about meeting a mountain lion in the wild. It's an irresistible impulse, this determination we have to impinge on their consciousness.

All this is very early thinking, at the brainstorming stage. The only way I know now to propose the book would be to say that I'd find the very best people to talk to about the subject, and ask how they understand animals. Ask each one, for example, "What's the smartest thing you've ever seen an animal do?" With luck, the book could be almost entirely anecdotal.

Working title, *Contacting Creatures, Creatures Contacting Us*. How we love animals: not how much we love them, but the ways in which we love them, the ways we find to love them.

Well. Not a book yet, but there's a book in there somewhere. Lots of thinking to be done. Better read up on St. Francis of Assisi.

••

Last night's subject doesn't seem quite so brilliant this morning, but it's a way into a subject that I'd like to spend time with. Think I'll see what the library has on Vilhjalmur Stefansson, check out this business about him and his dogs.

••

Two days after the equinox we get our first real fall weather, a nippy cold wind blowing all the crap out of the air, the visuals as crisp, clear, and sharp as they ever get. The dogs are full of beans, things are beginning to dry out.

I wear a down vest to walk the loop, and enjoy snuggling into it.

I ran into town selectman Bob Robertson, a longtime farmer, with whom I compared notes on the wetness of the summer. "A dry year will scare you to death," he said, "but a wet year will break you."

• •

This morning I had a long and soulful phone call from Dick Todd: Dan Okrent's resignation as editor of *New England Monthly* is now public, and Todd is under considerable pressure to take the job. He'd already decided not to, but no other decent candidate has been uncovered, and Okrent and the new owners are pressuring him to take it.

I wasn't surprised to get a call from him, thinking he'd heard that C. had sold her book and wanted details. But he seemed to be looking for support or encouragement, or just wanted to talk things over, which really was surprising. We'd never had anything like that direct and substantive a conversation before. C.'s opinion, I'm sure, would be earnest encouragement to take it, and I told him that—and then, as honestly as I could, gave him my own bleak view of magazines. After we finished talking, I wondered if he weren't also calling to sniff out whether C. would come back to work for him as managing editor.

C.'s customary evening call came a few minutes later, and I relayed as much of the conversation as I could. She said she'd call him immediately.

• •

Turned down another magazine assignment, one of those standard phone-some-authorities pieces. The editor asked if

I knew someone else who could do it, but I couldn't immediately come up with a name. Five minutes later I thought of
someone perfect for the assignment, so I called back and put
them onto her. Then I felt especially virtuous; I'd dodged an
assignment I'd have hated doing, and had done a favor for a
friend.

The piece was one I'd written ten times and couldn't
imagine finding interesting again. To do it without interest would be doing it just for the money, and I already know how poisonous that can be. I'm not too pure
to write for money, I just want to be entertained while I
do it.

• •

At dawn the wind seemed to be out of the east, promising
rain and bringing sweet fall smells down out of the meadow.
But it switched back into the north and west, and now, at two
in the afternoon, still no clouds. I was tempted—with perfect
justification—just to sit at the top of the field and look at
things, but kept walking. Turned into a great day, warm
enough for a T-shirt.

C. comes home tomorrow; I mailed off a chunk of this
manuscript to give my editor a first look, then did a gigantic
shopping, replacing groceries for C.'s return. I'm a regular
bundle of energy today, anticipating the return to connubial
bliss. In the matter of the optimum working day, and the
number of daily hours over which one can hope to be productive, I forgot to mention the short-row phenomenon: near
the end of a project the productive hours extend themselves
almost infinitely. Tasks which would ordinarily fog you out in
three or four hours can now be pursued for ten or twelve
hours straight. It sets in as soon as you can see the end of the

project. I doubt this phenomenon is exclusive to the writing trade.

• •

A perfect fall day, and C. got home about 11:00 a.m., three hours earlier than planned. In the best of all possible worlds there probably won't be many entries here for the next few days. See other book.

Of all fatiguing, futile, empty trades, the worst, I suppose, is
writing about writing. —Hilaire Belloc

• • • • • • • • • • • • • • • • • • • •

eavy fog this morning, the emerging reds and yellows of the foliage popping from the mist at dawn. I am trying to take in the woods without putting the word on them, no writing allowed. One sees better this way—but how does a writer make a living out of that?

So here it is October, we're both back at our desks, life resumes. C. returned from the Adirondacks full of great stories and solid research: a spectacularly productive time for her, not in small part I think because she was able, for a little while, to think of herself as a writer.

That's not an easy step for some of us, but once taken, the ravishing new project you then have going is called "writing," and, as with any good project, everything begins to connect to it. One's life becomes unexpectedly integrated.

I'm not sure why it's difficult to achieve this self-anointment; diffidence, I suppose. When I was publishing *Sports Car Digest,*

I hired a young man to sell ads, or at least that's what I thought he would do. He thought he would photograph and write about sports-car races. Before this misunderstanding was addressed I happened to accompany him as he was applying for credit at Sears. When he came to the blank for occupation, he asked me what he should put down, and then, before I could answer, entered the word "writer." I was outraged; at the time I'd never had the brass to claim that lofty designation for myself.

• •

Dick Todd has accepted the job as editor of *New England Monthly*. Great relief here that he is staying on. C. was the last person he talked to before making the decision.

I probably did more to talk him out of it than into it, expressing complete sympathy over the hassles and aggravation, the enormous energy drain that would go with the job. C. just gave him a hard time, saying hey, they're going to turn over the magazine to you and support you in it, what's the problem? He must've felt that we were doing a good-cop, bad-cop routine on him.

• •

Marty sends a magnificently frustrating bulletin about the publishing business. A friend asked him for editing help on a doctoral dissertation about post-Vietnam stress syndrome. Marty looked it over and told his friend it would make a trade book, that he ought to clean it up and send it around, get an agent. The grad student, who has never published anything, who needed help writing his thesis, did so—and the proposal sold for sixty-nine thousand dollars. Is subject matter everything or what?

. . . .

• •

The library in Northampton turns out to have quite a bit on Vilhjalmur Stefansson, in an unusually large collection, for such a small town, of polar literature. Rubbing of hands here. I checked out his autobiography, *Discovery* (1964—he died in 1976, in Vermont!). I also brought home the next volume on which my hand happened to fall, something he published in the twenties called *The Adventure of Wrangel Island,* just to see what this guy was up to.

• •

C.'s brother Mike called from Toronto this morning to tell her how much he liked her most recent column. When she told me this, my sole (and precisely wrong) reaction was to ask whether he'd ever received the copy of *Stone Work* I sent him, which seems to have gone astray in the mail. She pointed out that this was not exactly an appropriate response.

Alfred Lunt and Lynne Fontanne used to do a sketch in which they are making a movie. Lunt comes in from viewing the day's rushes, and Fontanne asks how they were. He was terrible, she was fine, Lunt says; her mouth looked a little funny in one scene, but otherwise she was perfect. He, on the other hand, is in despair, he can't go on. His work was rotten, the director is an idiot, his voice kept cracking, there's no pace and no wit in the piece, he has somehow forgotten how to act, he'll be disgraced if this footage ever sees the light of day.

"My mouth looked funny?" replies Fontanne.

• •

I've started reading *This Incomperable Lande,* a collection of American nature writing edited by Thomas J. Lyon. C. agreed to review it for *Countryside*—or, she told the editor, if she couldn't get to it she'd hand it over to me. She's busy, so I picked it up. *Countryside* will pay a dollar a word, and wants twelve hundred words. And it's a subject in which I'm quite interested.

Ten cents a word was the standard rate when I first began getting paid for writing. As with hourly wages, word rates invite abuse, but they're the only decent scale that writers and editors are likely to agree upon. Some publications pay by the published page, but that can be unfair to magazine as well as writer, since it sets payment in part on the basis of what the art director does with illustrations and decorative material.

When the bulk of my writing was for magazines, I argued that payment should be keyed to advertising rates, since those tend to be more reality-based than any of the other numbers the magazine deals with. I never got a publisher even to consider this idea. At this writing a dollar a word is what most new magazines of reasonable quality start out paying. It's a decent, even generous rate for writers, certainly. New magazines want writers to think well of them. Unfortunately, when production costs begin to rise, payment to writers is the first area to be scaled back.

A dollar a word says more about inflation than about publishing generosity, and it has taken a long time for rates to rise to that level. A former editor at *Playboy* once told a friend about negotiating with Norman Mailer and his agent when that publication's standard rate was twenty-five cents a word. They met in a Chicago bar, and the agent kept telling the editor how much literary class Mailer would add to the magazine. "Norman could describe the bottles behind that bar," the agent bragged, "and make it into a work of literature." Mailer, on the other hand, talked only about rate of payment:

he wanted to break the barrier, to be paid the then unheard-of sum of a dollar a word. "Well," the editor told him, "we'll pay a dollar for words like 'usufruct' and 'eleemosynary,' but not for every 'and,' 'but,' and 'the.' "

. .

Thirty Canada geese on the pond this morning; yesterday, sixty.

I spent that day in a borrowed truck, fetching the tractor from the shop: driving around the valley, racking up a hundred miles or so. The foliage season is upon us, and local roads are bumper to bumper, with tag sales and other diversions stacking traffic for miles in every direction. Afterward I realized that I'd driven *at* the task, fighting it, pressing to get it done. I was an actor; if I had been a spectator instead—if I had looked on it as entertainment instead of something I was forced to participate in—I'd have been diverted. It would have been different, perhaps even amusing. If I'd looked at the traffic jams as something to write about, I might have gotten interested in the process and enjoyed it. To lose the capacity to pull back and observe is to shirk my job. We are all characters in a comic novel, I mustn't forget that.

Yesterday was also one of those incompetent days when everything I touched broke off in my hand. At this time of year, I said to C., everything physical is rotting, and everything mechanical is breaking. "Can I have that line for a column?" she immediately asked.

I wasn't entirely joking. There are, I maintain, perfectly valid physical reasons why everything goes bad at this time of year, why light bulbs give up the ghost, appliances crash, batteries die. Faced with longer nights and shorter days, we are filled with urgency, going at everything too hard and too quickly, slapping at light switches and yanking on controls. Mechanical and electrical appliances are colder and drier, seals are brittle, flexibility reduced, liquids congealed, lubricants nonflowing. Tough time of the year. This is another thing I must try to remember.

• •

My unhealthy interest in such matters as rates of payment comes, I think, from entering the writing business from the impoverished underside: scrambling at it, doing whatever writing I could get paid for. I had no literary ambitions (that I'd admit), and in fact first got myself regularly into print by the simple expedient of starting my own publication. But I didn't own it, I had backers. Maybe I was in sales after all.

When one comes into the writing business from the bottom, magazines loom as the obvious mother lode of support. They can serve that purpose, but not easily. To earn a decent living from magazine writing alone is virtually impossible, requiring the equivalent of at least a major feature a month. Magazines serve more effectively not as subsidy but as a fairly rigorous school. Existing as they do in the commercial ruck, they teach very quickly what can be made to work and what can't. They put a mantle of practicality over one's wilder imaginings.

My version of magazine rates is surely out of date, and a little inaccurate: the going price is actually whatever the traffic will bear—and agents do a better job of getting fair money than writers can. This is particularly true of writers who have worked as editors and know the budgetary hell that editors regularly go through. Dan Okrent has paid fairly well at *NEM*, considering the size of the magazine, but did a manful job of holding the line against the escalating whine of the writers, myself among them. It is generally understood among editors, if not among writers, that freelancers could be paid more without materially affecting the overall budgetary picture of the magazine, but one has to hold the line somewhere.

The problem for magazines is that writers who do first-rate work are usually successful enough that money is not of first importance. If an assignment comes along that lets the writer explore a subject of true personal interest, or that gets him somewhere he wants to go, then he'll take it; otherwise, there are more productive ways to spend the time. Magazines therefore work more frequently with writers who definitely do need the money, who would like to get the rates raised so everyone can make a better living at this business. These writers are unfortunately seldom important enough to the magazines they write for to exert any real pressure. Myself among them.

· ·

No geese on the pond for the first time in a week. The woods, wet from the rain, are as sweet-smelling as they ever get, autumn woods with a new coat of brilliant yellow leaves on the floor, perfumed, Japanese-ly beautiful. Today proves once again that the time to look at fall foliage is when the sky is gray and the light low—at dawn, for instance.

I love to walk that early, but the best use of walking—for the work, if not for the soul—is not to get out at dawn but to rise from an extended bout at the desk and head for the door. To get immediately away from work, forgetting about it for ten minutes or so, then letting it roil back up to the surface of the mind. The result, usually, is new insights, new ideas, clearer phrasings. Sometimes I think I use walking as a way of getting away from the writing machine so I can think.

As with walking, so with talking with C., of course. If I try to tell her about something before I write it, it's not particularly useful. (For the same reason, I try to avoid pitching a story or book idea verbally—especially over the phone. That's always a disaster.) But if I leave off a draft that I've been working on all day, settle down with a drink and begin talking about something else entirely, the subject of the day's work eventually comes back around, and when it does it always seems to crack open in slightly different ways.

• •

In the matter of Vilhjalmur Stefansson, the good news is that he was a competent, readable writer. I started *The Adventure of Wrangel Island* first, intrigued by the enigmatic title, before tackling the autobiography. It's a curious story: Wrangel is a small island well above the Arctic Circle to which, at the turn of the century, Russia, Great Britain, and the United States had conflicting claims. It was uninhabited, but Stefansson hoped to colonize it for Canada and the British Empire, envisioning its eventual strategic significance as an Arctic air base. (Orville Wright was an early supporter.) The scheme was mounted by Stefansson, but he didn't join the expedition, staying south to organize funding and, he hoped, Canadian government support.

Four young white men and an Eskimo woman with the wonderful name of Ada Blackjack were landed on the island in 1921, intending to stay two years. The woman was employed as cook and seamstress, for the fine sewing necessary to maintain the skin clothing required for Arctic survival. Two years later, when a resupply ship managed to get to the island, only Ada Blackjack was still alive. Three of the men had disappeared while attempting to cross sea ice to Siberia, and the fourth had died of "starvation due to lack of game," according to the rescuer, a man named Harold Noice.

Later newspaper accounts, based on interviews with Noice,

grew more scandalous, claiming that Blackjack had demanded that one of the men marry her—any of them would do—and was spurned. She grew morose, stopped work, ceased cooperating. The three who died on the sea ice were going for supplies; after they didn't return, the fourth became ill with scurvy and could no longer hunt. Rather than nursing the ailing man, according to the newspapers, Blackjack had withheld food for herself, causing his death by starvation.

This version, however, was based on diaries that Noice had confiscated and shown to no one. While the journals were in his possession he erased entries and even tore out pages. When the reports began to reflect badly on everyone concerned, pressure was brought to produce the journals, which, even edited, didn't jibe with his account. Eventually Noice recanted, apologizing to the families of the dead men, claiming that an impending "severe attack of nervous prostration" had affected his judgment.

Thus the "Adventure," which Stefansson wrote to clear his own name as well as those of the people in his employ. The text quivers with righteous indignation, and is largely devoted to the argument that Wrangel Island is a hospitable place, more suitable for development than many Arctic sites. Some of Stefansson's version doesn't add up. According to samples from the recovered diaries, for example, Ada Blackjack did undergo a spell of considerable psychological disturbance.

Whatever actually happened on Wrangel Island, one truth emerges: expeditions, and expeditionary journals, make great reading.

• •

Last night we were talking about one-liners, in the comedy-writing sense—and it occurred to me that actors also speak of lines. "Line" is slang for sentence. A good gag line has all the qualities you're looking for in a sentence. Every sentence doesn't have to be a gag line, but every sentence can have the tension and balance and economy of good comedy writing— plain good writing, in other words.

Writers may not admit it, but some part of us is always looking for the line that will be repeated, that will stay alive and get quoted. Maybe this derives from television's compression of the attention span, making aphorists of us all.

Talking to C. about lines, I remarked what a powerful invention the sentence is. Punctuation, too, she says; the Romans and Greeks didn't have it, and language was amazingly clumsy without it. The image that comes to me is a toolbox: punctuation is nails, screws, nuts and bolts, the means by which you secure things in place, maintain the space (time) between them, put the rhythm into sentences so they become comprehensible. Punctuation as fastener.

. .

I am baking cookies. There is lettering around the lid of the Crisco can: DO NOT EXPOSE CAN TO HEAT OR REFILL WITH HOT OIL. *That*'s the way I want to write. That, students, is fine writing.

. .

Clipping old magazines, for sources of ideas for future *Log*s, sets me reflecting on my cynicism about the magazine business. I grew up with magazines—in my school years I read every issue of the old weekly *Life, Collier's,* and *Saturday Evening Post*—but I became actively interested in them only by way of automobiles. In college I went a little car-crazy and started reading automobile magazines. They actually tested products, about which they had daring things to say, hinting that they

206

would reveal the truth about goods on the market. I found this exciting, a kind of honesty unavailable in other periodicals. It appealed to the writer in me: a chance to lay about with the sword of truth, and all that romantic nonsense.

In the real world of magazines such honesty is seldom possible. Most of the time if you even hint that a product is a dubious value, the manufacturer pulls, or threatens to pull, his advertising. Then your publisher, who is the business head of your enterprise, jumps on your case. You are asked, albeit gingerly, to apologize, to produce make-up stories, to lard your pages with favorable mentions. ("Editorial integrity" is a phrase that will never be uttered.) I thought for years that this was only the case in special-interest magazines, but it happens even in magazines that weren't created to talk about products. When Harold Hayes gave up two pages of *Esquire* to men's toiletries, that was only a small, ancient version of what continues to go on in any medium that carries advertising.

It is difficult for the writer to keep in mind that magazines are created not to dispense information or even to entertain but to carry advertising. Special-interest magazines are created to carry advertising for the products that are used in that special interest, and in fact their editorial material is largely free advertising, only slightly disguised as journalism about those products. Knocking the products is therefore a dubious course. But how to maintain the sense that you're telling the truth? The answer is to pick your targets. I was working at a car magazine when Studebaker finally went under, and I remember the glee with which we fell on the news: now, since they wouldn't be advertising anymore, we could finally say what terrible automobiles they had been foisting off on the public for all those years. Verisimilitude is what makes a hot magazine. It gets readers interested. It is, by definition, lying.

In the slightly more dignified world of general-interest media, including television, the big advertisers are reluctant to throw their weight around for fear of getting tarred with the free-speech brush. So the advertisers arrive at a gentleman's agreement with the media: you refrain from practicing free speech about our products, and we'll refrain from practicing free markets by withdrawing our advertising.

• •

I've been thinking back about C.'s notion of *The Farm,* about how that idea seized us both at the time, about the thrill, the invigoration, of dealing with strong ideas.

When one of these ideas comes, the feeling is almost as if you're remembering it; it has always been there, but something makes the coin drop. It is something you've been thinking about all along, but thinking with some hitherto unavailable part of your mind. The idea is there waiting to be exposed; getting it is simply a matter of discovering what that part of your mind is really thinking about.

I keep saying the idea drops; more likely it rises, from the metaphorical nether regions, but in any case it just appears. Maybe this is a definition of the muse.

• •

The mail brings catalog copy for the paperback of *Stone Work,* to be issued next July—a little reminder that life goes on, and no book lasts forever. Eight thousand four hundred and seventy-nine copies of the hardback have now been shipped, only three hundred more than last May.

Willy bitches because he wasn't reviewed in the *Times* and a couple of other crucial places. I point out that my book was reviewed everywhere that his wasn't, and ends up selling fewer copies. This does not make him feel better.

· ·

Indian summer holds. The dogs are absolutely full of joy in this weather, with new fall smells and all the wildlife in motion. Their joy is infectious, making them a treat to be with: birdy, full of enthusiasm. They are not depressed; they pull me along through the woods and put a little extra joy in my life too.

The unfortunates on Wrangel Island used dogs, but the dogs don't figure in the story. Stefansson's autobiography, *Discovery*, also mentions dogs from time to time—he complains about native treatment of the animals, praises some individual dogs he worked with, confirms that he'd never eat one—but the dog connection is not a significant theme in the book.

It's an entertaining read, however. Stefansson comes off as a bumptious character, somehow characteristic of the twenties, attempting to sell grand Arctic schemes to various governments, pursuing oddball dietary theories. He seems mostly to have had a particular talent for living off the land, learning the Eskimo dialects, living comfortably and harmoniously with the aboriginal people. People who do that come back with fewer tales to tell, because heroics are seldom required. "Adventure is a sign of incompetence," Stefansson says. That may be part of the reason he never made a big splash as an Arctic explorer: he was too good at it.

New England Monthly's last page carries a standing feature called "Minor Details," usually a selection of obscure facts about some New England character. Since Stefansson ended up at Dartmouth—to which he sold his voluminous Arctic

. . . .

library—it occurred to me to try to fit the man into that format, maybe sell a little one-pager:

HE NEVER ATE HIS DOGS
Vilhjalmur Stefansson, 1879–1962

1. He changed his name from William to Vilhjalmur while he was in college, to honor his Icelandic heritage.

2. He was admitted to Harvard Divinity School but only as an anthropologist, studying religion as folklore.

3. He spent more years in the Arctic—twelve—than any other polar explorer, including Peary.

4. He once carried a two-hundred-pound bearskin, head, and paws for twenty miles overland on his back.

5. He discovered a tribe of previously unknown Eskimos, which he mistakenly characterized to the press as blond-haired and blue-eyed, doing serious damage to his scientific reputation as a result.

6. As an experiment he once lived for a year on a supervised diet of eighty percent animal fat and twenty percent lean meat. This was not a hardship, as his favorite meal had always been boiled mutton and the broth thereof—without salt. He died at eighty-three, not from the cardiac infarction that all that fat should have brought on, but from a stroke that his salt-free diet should have helped prevent.

7. The only man he ever trusted in the Arctic, R. M. Anderson, turned on him at the start of their second expedition, and devoted the rest of his life to vilifying him, attempting to convince the world that Stefansson was a charlatan.

8. He broke with Arctic tradition and treated his dogs well, refusing to eat them—although he cheerfully ate anything else he could kill, and considered wolf an excellent dish.

9. He pointed out that running out of fuel in the Arctic

means dying of thirst, not hunger: one is surrounded by water in its useless solid state.

10. After his Arctic days he sold half of his Vermont farm to Owen Lattimore. Joe McCarthy's minions immediately began investigating him, in part because he also happened to be married to a woman who had actually studied Russian—in order to translate Russian Arctic literature for his polar library, now at Dartmouth.

Too many items, and I can't choose among them for zaniness. Most of them are on Stefansson's own say-so, and need to be checked further. Looks like I have a trip to Dartmouth ahead of me.

. .

Heavy rains last night turn the loop into a stream this morning, a wade instead of a walk. We're just about halfway through the foliage season, but the impact and weight of the rain has materially accelerated its end—slipping little sash weights into the leaves' knapsacks, encouraging their fall, packing them more tightly into the mulch. I find it comforting to think that the same six-inch layer that autumn drops on our local hillside is also being dropped on the umpteen million other acres of deciduous forest in the northern hemisphere.

The rains do tend to overachieve. Gravity gathers up strands of water here and rivulets there, braiding them, cutting miniature new streambeds through the duff. The leaves are washed up into dikes, making tiny canyon walls alongside the rivulets' flow, gathering into occasional small dams complete with minuscule millponds above and spillways below. Kames and eskers. The rivulet beds are dark clay furrows, arrows pointing down the hillside, schematic diagrams of gravity.

211

These furrows set me worrying about erosion—but then on a hillside, one never ceases worrying about erosion.

• •

Stefansson on dietary matters:

Sir Robert Borden suggested that I go at once to England to enlist the aid of Lord Strathcona, Canada's High Commissioner. Strathcona . . . was over ninety but still active, and one of the richest men in the British Empire. . . .
. . . there grew up between us the bond of a common interest—an interest in dietary matters. I told him what I had learned from the Eskimos, and he told me that years ago in Canada he had begun a regimen of his own by skipping lunch and ultimately breakfast too. Then he had begun to wonder why, since he liked some things better than others, he should bother to eat something different on Tuesday when he had liked what he had eaten on Monday better. This led to his questioning what he really did like and, when he got the answer, eating nothing else—eggs, milk, and butter. Although this combination would not have made up my favorite meal, much as I favor butter, the point was that Strathcona and I were in agreement on the feeling that the longer a man ate one complete food exclusively, the more likely he was to relish it.
. . . he frequently invited me to dinner at his home in Grosvenor Square. . . . Strathcona, a broad-shouldered man taller than six feet, would be seated at one end of the long table, Lady Strathcona at the other. As course after course was served to the rest of us, he would converse, drinking a sip or two of each wine as it was poured. Sometime during the middle of the dinner, his tray was brought: several medium-soft boiled eggs broken into a large bowl, with plenty of butter and with extra butter in a side dish, and, I believe, a quart of whole milk, or

perhaps half-and-half. My impression is that they also brought him toast, but that he barely nibbled it, using it a bit as if it were a napkin.

. .

Jonathan Raban's jaundiced view of journalism coincides curiously with Barry Lopez's similar criticism of official geographies: "covering" a subject by laying a grid down on it, rather than learning the lay of the land. The journalist's job is to go in and get a broad understanding, to learn enough of the terminology to speak knowledgeably, to be able quickly to understand the situation and do the story. The better a journalist is at this quick study, the more he will be able to do, the more money he will make, the more spectacularly his career will advance. And the more hollow his work will be.

One year *Skiing* assigned a piece about the trees on ski slopes. I turned it into a two-parter, eastern slopes one issue, western slopes the next. For the series I learned to identify all the trees one might run across on a ski mountain anywhere in the United States, and wrote a short-form field guide, with all the identifying characteristics, so any skier who bothered could do the same.

Two years later, a tree that was too close to the house needed removal. We called the local arborist to do the job. As he was preparing to go to work, I asked him what kind of tree it was. Maple, he replied.

A depressingly high percentage of the people who make a living from writing do so in this world of the quick take. I don't want to anymore, which is another reason I resist magazine work.

. .

Journalism on the road: In 1974, returning from a travel assignment in the Midwest, I catch a Friday-afternoon commuter flight that makes stops in Traverse City, Grand Rapids, Kalamazoo, and South Bend, gathering salesmen back to Chicago for the weekend. The flight is empty when I get on. I take the window of a banquette just behind the bulkhead and open a book. As the flight fills it is clear that I am blocking a card game among regulars, but by then there are no other seats.

After a while the guy across from me kicks my foot under the table—rather harder than necessary—and says, aggressively, "You a peddler?"

No, I say noncommittally, and return to my book. What do I do? Writer. Oh, who do you write for? *Time? Esquire? Playboy?* No, I'm a freelance, I say. "Oh," says my interrogator, *"you're* a peddler."

• •

Dinner last night at Dan and Becky Okrent's, with, among others, Jim Gaines, editor of *Life,* former editor of *People.* The evening provided an extended dialogue with Gaines and Okrent—or, more accurately, between them, since I pretty well stayed out of it—on the subject of magazines vs. books. Dan, who worked in book publishing before starting *NEM,* likes the magazine business more than the book business, in part because the writer receives much more editing in magazines than in books. The goal of writing is to be read, he said, and editing makes writing more readable.

No, said Gaines, as far as the writer is concerned the goal of writing is to get it said, and readership should be left to find itself. Not too surprisingly, I found myself thinking that perhaps I ought to try to sell something to Gaines.

A part of Dan's disappointment with the book business has to do with the industry's calm acceptance of the fact that ninety-eight percent of its effort is spent on two percent of the books—which from the writer's point of view certainly seems to be true. He also makes a strong case that a great number of the books being published today don't get edited at all. A retiring copy editor at a major house recently told C. that some editors don't edit at all, never touch the manuscript —they leave all that to the copyediting department.

I bitch a lot about the publishing business, but this has not been a complaint of mine.

· ·

Listened to some literary talk show on the car radio the other day, and one of the panelists noted that every word is a metaphor, all words are metaphors. Not a terribly original observation, but it struck home: here we are with the capacity for language, the tool with which we've built this incredible civilization. And yet the capacity for language itself specifically freezes us at the symbolic level, permanently divorced from the experience of the real world. We are incurably afloat in a sea of words, of symbolic representation, and can't cut through to the thing itself. It is the Word that makes us so powerful, and that prevents us from seeing the actuality that the Word represents.

A man receives only what he is ready to receive, whether physically or intellectually or morally, as animals conceive at certain seasons their kind only. We hear and apprehend only what we already half know. . . . Every man thus tracks himself through life, in all his hearing and reading and observation and travelling. His observations make a chain. The phenomenon or fact that cannot in any wise be linked with the rest of what he has observed, he does not observe. By and by we may be ready to receive what we cannot receive now. —Henry David Thoreau

N O V E M B E R

• • • • • • • • • • • • • • • • • •

*G*ray, cold, *very* November, the woods wet and brown and beautiful, sweet-smelling. With the foliage down we can now see the lights of town (and the occasional junked car). And what's this, sounds of a goose flight, on November 6? Thought they were long gone; hope they're coming to the pond. If you aren't moved by that sound there is no hope for you.

Dripping honey onto a biscuit at breakfast the other day, I repeated a corny old family joke about the slowness of the process, and then was swept by the memory of how bored I was, growing up, with all those family sayings and stories, how necessary it was to reject all that, walk away from it. How— see *Place*—I had to shake the dust of that burg off my heels. How inevitably one opts for the new, tries it, tries it all, and finds that none of it works, the new being such an exhausting way to fulfill, or even entertain, oneself.

And now, at my age—on this day, which happens to be the last of my fifty-seventh year—it is the return of the old that seems fresh. As in the return of the geese. What one wants is not the new but the re-newed, to find a way of re-newing. You want to find a way to see freshly what has become unbearably old, the very things that drove you away (from home? from the place?) to start with.

. .

This morning C. spotted a deer eating windfall apples by the dog pen, not thirty yards from the house; now, at two in the afternoon, I look for more—in a heavy fog, visibility a hundred yards and shrinking as the dogs and I climb the hill. I don't really want to see any: this is bow-hunting season. Maybe the fog will hide the deer.

Today's mail brought the worst review I ever received, in *Boston* magazine. The reviewer said that for someone to write a book about building a stone wall and then to get it published represents the end of civilization as we know it. My immediate impulse was to write to her saying, By God you're right, I am withdrawing the book and shall stop writing. But Tracy Kidder gets rough treatment in the same piece, so I will try to cheer up, finding myself in good company.

. .

As I struggle with these book proposals, I'm trying to think about the work I want to do instead of how the hell I am going to finance it. This is a great relief. I've got to find a way to produce work good enough to finance itself. I must focus on making the work better, not on what somebody out there will buy—or, worse, what I hypothesize that somebody out there will buy. I've tried that other way with too many books, and it doesn't work. I'm too old, I don't have enough time. If I'm going to do anything worthwhile with my writing, I have to push on through to the next step. The next step is not yet another of these pathetic attempts to discern and supply what the public can be tricked into purchasing.

Hello, I seem to be working myself into another rage. It is surely in frustration at not being able to come up with a big idea. This morning's *Times Book Review* has a piece by Diane Ackerman, excerpted from a coming book about the senses. I've had a book on that subject working in the back of my mind for years, but it never jelled, I never came up with a way to do it. Judging from this excerpt I couldn't have written it nearly as well. Pure jealousy: a few years ago I gave a cover blurb for Ackerman's book about learning to fly. Helping out the new kid. Ever since I have been watching her shoot past me into *The New Yorker* and other prestigious markets.

As a young reader, when you come across a writer who speaks personally to you, you think, Thank God there's someone else in the world who understands. As you get older and read someone who sees things as you see them, you think, *I could've said that.* Damn, I could've thought that, I could've had that insight.

I hate the Big Idea approach. It is saving *Esquire*'s October all over again. Or I hate the Big Idea approach until I have one.

Anger, they say, shows you where you're stuck. This morning I seem to be stuck on money and success.

· ·

Browsing in the library, C. happened across *The Arctic Grail*, by Pierre Berton. She checked it out for me, thinking it might fit my plans. Boy, does it ever. The subtitle is *The Quest for the North West Passage and the North Pole, 1818–1909:* a survey of nearly a hundred years of exploration, and I am eating it up. I opened it this morning with my coffee, and ideas started to pop; I began making mental notes even as I was brushing my teeth. There is such joy in that kind of work, and I'd virtually forgotten it for days now, brooding over my so-called career. Now, says my brain with a giggle of relief, back to work.

The same thing happened to C. during negotiation for her book contract. She was in the Adirondacks, having a fine time chasing down leads, when the negotiations began to get fruitful. For two or three days she found herself unable to do anything but hang around the phone, worrying about how the deal-making was going. She couldn't get her head free of the details of financing the work in order to get on with the work.

· ·

Opening *The Arctic Grail*, I flipped first to the index to look up Vilhjalmur Stefansson. There were only two entries, the first of which mentioned briefly that both Peary and Stefansson took native mistresses. I read the line and slapped myself on the forehead. Of course. The Wrangel Island mystery explained: "seamstress" indeed. Thus Stefansson's contentment at those twelve long years in the Arctic. I am so naïve.

As Berton sees it, all Arctic exploration starts with Sir John Franklin, and is fueled thereafter by the search either for his remains or for the elusive Northwest Passage, the Arctic Grail of the title. Franklin's first expedition had been "a human disaster; his second was worthy but uninspiring; his third ended in a dreadful tragedy, the worst the Arctic had ever seen": the loss of two ships and a hundred and twenty-nine men.

"None of this mattered to the Victorians," writes Berton, "who were captivated by noble failure, as Tennyson's paean to an extraordinary piece of military bungling had demonstrated. It didn't matter whether you won or lost, it was how you played the game; and Franklin, his memory kept alive and sanctified by his widow, was seen to have played it out according to the rules, dashing forward into the Arctic labyrinth, like the doomed cavaliers of the Light Brigade, an enthusiastic amateur to the last."

The second entry for Stefansson pursues this point. Berton is obsessed with the mulishness of the British Navy, which seems never to have learned anything from a hundred years of polar tragedies, mindlessly repeating their predecessors' mistakes. "The most iconoclastic of the twentieth-century explorers, Vilhjalmur Stefansson, damned them with a bitter epitaph. They died, he wrote, because they brought their environment with them; they were not prepared and had not learned how to adapt to another.

"In this, of course, they were the creatures of their age. All over the globe in the outposts of Empire, pukka sahibs were continuing to live as if the countryside of Wordsworth was at their back door, apparently oblivious to climate and culture, secure in their conviction that the English form of civilization was the only form."

I love this stuff.

• •

One of the very few things that have been wrong with this year is that it has kept me producing far too fast. I've pumped

220

and pumped out the words, letting writing go long before it was ready. Next year must provide a chance to slow down, get the writing right. That's the reason for working on new book proposals at this early stage.

This means getting a new book contract to buy time to finish up the book on hand, thereby mortgaging one book's writing time in order to complete the other. It's a dubious proposition, but the only way at hand. Besides, to research one book while grooming and tightening another is not only possible, it can be positively stimulating.

· ·

I'm trying to get a handle on my recent ill temper at the publishing business. It is hardly fair—the business is supporting me, after all—but I can't seem to rationalize my way out of it. I didn't set out to vent fury over these matters, but if that's what comes through, it surely indicates that, at my level of competence anyway, the writer's life is not unaffected by this particular anger. Every writer I know expresses it, one way or another, even those who are making commercial successes of their work. The rest of us, our noses pressed against the glass, suffer from the delusion that if we come up with the Big Idea we'll be admitted to the club. Part of our rage is from watching, along with some very large and estimable talents, all these slicksters and con men who cart off obscene amounts of money for unreadable and meretricious products, while we bend over our washboards.

The publishing industry would surely say that my rage shouldn't be at it but at the nonbuying, uncaring public. The publishing industry is probably right, but that's their rage too—not uncommonly expressed in cynical and contemptuous attempts to manipulate the market.

The publishing industry is ashamed of itself; you feel it

everywhere. But then the media business in general is ashamed of itself (as we writers in it are ashamed of ourselves). Certainly TV and the movies are ashamed of themselves. The television news business is ashamed of itself, and getting more shamefaced every day. Newspapers are. And let's not even talk about advertising.

Gee, and Amanda Vaill says the view in this manuscript is getting a little "bleak."

• •

I'm so swept up in *The Arctic Grail* that I didn't even turn on the machine yesterday. Todd is supposed to call soon to talk about editing changes to the New Hampshire piece, which process I look forward to. I have that revision to do, the book review of *This Incomperable Lande,* and—except for keeping up with this journal—that's it for the rest of the year. Unless a book proposal idea clicks into place, and I get swept up in writing that.

• •

C. pointed out last night, accurately, I think, that books of the sort that I write are unlikely ever to sell more than eight thousand copies, and I shouldn't keep pushing at it. I should instead figure out how to live on eight-thousand-copy sales. She's certainly right, and I should keep that firmly in mind. But I don't know if I can ever stop lunging for the larger prize.

What we don't realize, she says, is that this—our lives now, the way we live—is the jackpot. She's right, as usual.

• •

The "real" books I write sell eight thousand copies; Random House manages, year after year, to sell sixty to seventy thousand copies of the *Runner's Log*. What's wrong with this picture?

. .

When C. worked at *NEM*, employees who resigned were asked to turn over their Rolodexes. The information they contained was valuable reference material, gathered under the auspices of the magazine. Matter of policy. There was no embargo against making personal take-home copies.

I carry into the reading of *Grail* the question of what went wrong between Stefansson and Anderson, only to realize that on expeditions something always goes wrong. There will always be terrible tensions, feuds, ruptures between the members. Being cramped into small spaces for long periods of time under stressful conditions understandably brings disputes to a head. It is the nature of expeditions.

Most expeditions do not reveal their disputes, in part because expedition contracts usually specify that all journals and diaries are under the leader's control. Only carefully edited versions are published. It is when the matter of publication comes up that the Rolodexes get embargoed; that's when you get "see other book," the deliciously informative journals that never get exposed. The juiciest expedition literature remains private.

The British Navy dealt with these tensions and stresses with, among other things, shipboard theatricals, for which they brought along costumes and musical instruments. (This was in addition to some surprising other impedimenta. Berton inventories one sledge, loaded for a desperate escape: it contained "every kind of footgear from sea boots to strong shoes, towels and toothbrushes, gun covers and twine, soap and sheet lead, dinner knives, crested silver plate, pocket watches and tools, a bead purse, a cigar case—everything in short that civilized nineteenth-century travellers considered necessary for their comfort and well-being.")

The Norwegians, on the other hand, brought dogs. On Amundsen's long voyage to the Antarctic, "the dogs were the great diversion," writes Roland Huntford, in *The Last Place on Earth*. "More than the men, they fill the diaries on board. Sometimes it almost seems as if the Norwegians found most of their companionship among the dogs. At any rate, the animals were a safety valve, stopping many a feud." When it was impossible to bear another moment of their human companions, the men could always turn and spend time with the dogs.

• •

Todd suggests only a few changes to the New Hampshire piece. I should take out the references to Hans and Lynne (they're introduced as characters but never function as such). I should cut the line about wanting to tell more stories about people (don't tease; as soon as I said that, Todd wanted me to tell the stories). I went back over the manuscript this morning, made those changes easily, cleaned up a couple of other paragraphs, and it's done. Cut about a hundred and fifty words. I'd been expecting a four- or five-day stint of anguished rewriting.

• •

We woke to a rim of ice around the pond and half an inch of snow on the deck—the first of the year, producing some delicious feline double takes when the cats went out for their morning constitutional.

Mostly today I am relieved to have the New Hampshire

· · · · · · · · · · · · · ·

piece edited and out of the way so easily. I'm impressed with Todd's sound reasons for the changes he wanted; he definitely gives the feeling that he's thought the changes through before asking for them, which is as much as a writer can ask. He doesn't suggest a change until he's figured out a way you can do it. He's so clear about his wishes that to disagree feels irrational.

· ·

Winter is here: howling winds all night, spitting snow at dawn, low twenties.

Yesterday was instructive. I went through the New Hampshire piece again in the morning, printed it off, got it ready to deliver. A Fed-Ex had arrived from Billy Sims at *Special Reports*, wanting a minor fix and a reference for fact-checking, so after dropping off the manuscript, I swung by the library and dug the reference out of *Reader's Guide*. Met Willy for lunch, came home, and just as I was about to take the dogs around the loop, Sims called, so I said I'd call back when I had the necessary fix written. Picked up the tape recorder, walked the loop dictating lines for the fix, phoned them in. Fed the dogs, read for ten minutes, fell asleep, woke up thirty minutes later at exactly five-thirty, time for the news. A smugly satisfying high-output day, only about twenty minutes of which was spent actually writing anything.

· ·

I am nostalgic these days for the powerful pleasure of a working rhythm, of getting settled into a pattern that allows large blocks of uninterrupted hours. Switching back and forth from project to project (as in earning a living) fragments time miserably. It is a relief now and then to be able to change topics, but when the work is going well, to be forced to switch back to some potboiler is the damnedest frustration. What's needed to produce a solid body of work is a solid body of time.

Not that I don't invent errands, keep myself distracted, use trips to town as escape hatches when the work isn't going well—and sometimes when it is, when I'm tired, when fatigue sets in. But the unbroken expanse of time is clearly where the good work comes from. At the writer's colony C. discovered that to have everything taken care of, to *be* taken care of and therefore to have time to work, is one of the most valuable gifts a writer can be given.

• •

The Arctic Grail has me bringing expedition stories downstairs to tell at dinnertime. For instance, Dr. Elisha Kent Kane, an American who became the best-known explorer of his day. He was medical officer on an American expedition searching for Franklin in 1850–1851, and wrote a highly romanticized account of the trip, which made him famous. In 1853 he went back to the Arctic as commander of a second expedition.

Between his first and second Arctic trips, Kane fell in love with nineteen-year-old Margaret Fox, who with her younger sister, Katherine, was a founder of the cult of spiritualism. They were "spirit-rappers," producing loud cracks from their toe joints that were interpreted as communications from the dead. Over a million Americans joined their movement. Kane saw the Fox sisters in Philadelphia in 1852, fell instantly in love with Margaret, and was determined to save her from a life of bunkum. He persuaded her to give up spirit rapping, installed her in a boardinghouse, with chaperone, at his expense, then left for the Arctic.

Kane's public reputation was for brilliant leadership, but he had never before captained a ship, knew little of navigation, and was constantly seasick. He was a "snobbish, overbearing, boastful" martinet who abused his officers and curried favor with the men, who obeyed him only when they felt like it. His ship was bound in ice for two desperate winters off the coast of Greenland. He was robbed by Eskimos and robbed them back, kidnapped women and imprisoned them on his ship, exchanged hostages and traded hardware for food, attempted to murder a rebellious crew member (but missed), was reviled and hated by his crew, who mutinied against him at regular intervals over the course of the two winters.

Finally, in the spring after the second winter, Kane and his men dragged three small boats for three hundred miles over ice and snow, launched them, fought blizzards, pack ice, and bergs for forty-nine days, ran out of food, burned the oars and sled runners for fuel. After eighty-four days in open air they were rescued. Only three men had perished in the two years, however, and Kane came home a bigger hero than ever. He paid his sailing master three hundred and fifty dollars to suppress a journal of the trip.

Maggie Fox awaited him in New York on his return, but Kane dodged her, in part because of his wealthy and adamantly disapproving Philadelphia family. (There was no mention of Margaret in either his private journal or published memoirs.) When they met again, Fox wanted to marry, but Kane kept putting her off. She dropped him, he asked her to take him back, they argued over who was dropping whom. Finally Kane, his heart already damaged by rheumatic fever, went to England to help Lady Franklin promote another search mission. There his precarious health took a turn for the worse; he sailed for Cuba, where he died—a "Great Explorer, Ripe Scholar and Noble Philanthropist." The only thing he accomplished in the Arctic, other than the loss of three men, was posting a "farthest north" by a white man.

Margaret Fox claimed that on the evening of his departure for England he asked that they pledge their troth before witnesses, including her mother, and they did. She published his love letters posthumously. "Remember then," she said, "as a sort of dream, that Doctor Kane of the Arctic Seas loved Maggie Fox of the spirit rappings."

Now there's a biography to write—or a movie.

• •

Expeditions, maybe that's the book. I should stop mooning over Stefansson—although he's definitely a quirky character, and there are these little mysteries surrounding him. Who was he really, a promoter and charlatan or a legitimate scientist? It would be great fun to try to exhume the trail, balance out the account. Unfortunately, as a book it'd be guaranteed to sell about five hundred copies.

But now I've become so intrigued by the quality of expedition stories, by the expedition mentality, that it occurs to me that a better book might be about expeditions in general. I could still use Stefansson as a thread to tie it together, a device for ranging through the history of exploration. It wouldn't be a survey like Berton's, which is perfectly admirable in itself, but an entirely capricious look at this form of human endeavor.

Amusingly enough, even the most respected explorers turn out to be more or less fly-by-night promoters; they have to be, to finance their expeditions. They also all seem more or less to lie about what they did, where they went. Claims of Peary, Cook, and now even Byrd have recently been exposed as dubious. Stefansson's nemesis, R. M. Anderson, claimed that Stefansson simply lived in an Eskimo village for a few years, then came out with outlandish stories about having gone all over the Arctic. Maybe none of them ever went anywhere. They seem to bring back a load of secrets, then let out exactly what they want, and no more. See other book.

Then there are the British, famous as a nation for inventing sports at which the rest of the world proceeds to thrash them soundly. In exploration they held firmly to this tradition, inventing a kind of expeditionary sportsmanship—a bunch of crazy rules, one of which seems to have been not to pay any attention to whatever it was that killed the fellow who tried it just before you. (Stefansson himself characterized exploration as a kind of international sporting contest.) The British also accomplished few of the quasi-scientific or geographical goals they attempted. Other nationalities came along, approached the task practically, and did the job: Norwegians at the South Pole, Americans at the North, a New Zealander on Everest.

Oh, this is fun. *Expeditions*. A kind of nonfiction *Ragtime*. Use *Great Plains* as a model. No, use Evan S. Connell's *Son of the Morning Star*. Start with the somewhat academic adventure of discovering whether Stefansson was a tinhorn promoter or a legitimate anthropologist/explorer. There's one expedition, right there. (Where are the scholarly papers? Are there scholarly papers?) Use that to open the subject of expeditions, the expedition process, the expedition mentality. (And have some fun with the art, or discipline, of biography along the way.) Throw in other expeditions like tall tales, brief summaries that pluck incidents out of the wider history. I wouldn't need to tell complete stories, but could select wonderful anecdotes out of them, wonderful lines, wonderful developments. Pull out only the wry, the unexpected, the illustrative moment when implacable Nature comes up against some screwball aspect of human character and something interesting develops. Throw in a story whenever an element of Stefansson's life triggers a connection.

There are fifty different expeditions described in *The Arctic Grail,* and that's just for the Arctic; there are also the Antarctic, the Alps, the Himalaya, Africa. Lewis and Clark, Stanley and Livingston, Powell, Pike. Not to mention Odysseus. This furrow is obviously well plowed, but not the way I'd do it. Anyway, I don't think I'll have a problem finding material.

• •

Critical response to *Stone Work* most often mentions the October chapter, which was the one with which I had the most trouble. I rewrote it completely three or four times after the rest of the book was done, throwing out whole sections, rediscovering—only after endless stewing—what the hell I was driving at. Judging by the reaction, that was one of the most successful parts of the book. It makes me feel virtuous that the struggle paid off.

Rewriting is as hard to describe as writing itself. In first drafts I tend to italicize words, trying to make them work harder: shouting to get the point across. One early step is simply to go through and recast the sentence to make italics unnecessary. This can often be done with intensifiers: "one does do a lot of rewriting," rather than, more simply, "one does a lot of rewriting." Intensifiers put little rockers in the sentence, kicking the emphasis into the right place in the structure. The next step is to discover how to dispense with the intensifiers. If the sentence is built well it will hit effectively without needing tricks.

The job of writing is in fact rewriting, which is the oldest

· · · · · · · · · · · · ·

cliché—and the deepest truth—in the business. I enjoy it most when the manuscript is long by about ten percent, and I can try to get it back down to length by nothing more than pulling sentences taut. That's when I finally find out what the sentences are trying to say. Some prove to be saying nothing at all, and go out the window. (I save them electronically—or anal-retentively—by throwing them into a temporary SCRAP file. Maybe they contain the germ of an idea that'll go somewhere else.) There is the mortifying but somehow entirely satisfactory feeling that comes when what looks like a cuttable phrase turns out to be a cuttable sentence, and then a cuttable paragraph. (Or section, or chapter. Do you realize, I always say to myself, how long it took to write that?) If I'm going to find a way to kick the manuscript up to another level, this is the stage at which I'll be able to do it.

Of course this discounts what the rewrite process is really for: to remove the mistakes, stupidities, errors and lapses of taste, mistaken interpretations, hasty impressions. The idiocies. Can't ever catch them all, but one has to keep trying.

· ·

Mailed off the review of *This Incomperable Lande,* not an entirely happy piece of writing. I found myself floundering in a kind of bogus-academic style, perhaps in response to Lyon's scholarship. The early writers—Bartram, Godman, Nuttall, even Audubon—are a snore, but the collection begins to get interesting along about Thoreau. He comes off in Lyon's selections as something of an ad man, a sloganeer for wildness, but there's a clear change of consciousness with him that informs all the writing that follows.

I suppose I also struggled because I've wanted to get into this Nature Club for some time now and have never quite figured out how. The natural world is for me the happiest possible subject about which to write. Reviewing the field gave me a chance to praise heroes—Matthiessen, Dillard, Lopez—and pan some of the more tiresome plonkers (Henry Beston; Donald Culross Peattie and other notorious three-namers; Loren Eisely). I found Rachel Carson the most impressive pure writer of the group, and quoted her extensively, perhaps because I discovered to my horror that I'd never read her (and pulled down *The Sea Around Us* for immediate attention). And I came away from a fairly intensive reading of the entire book remembering clearly only a single, arrow-straight simile by Edward Hoagland, from his essay "Hailing the Elusive Mountain Lion": a leopard drops from a tree "as heavy as a chunk of iron wrapped in a flag."

I didn't say so in the review, but that line gave me a nice few moments, thinking of the little surge of joy that must have pulsed through Hoagland's mind when the image occurred to him. How his eyes must have widened, momentarily, with wonder, at that amazing little gift that came from God knows where.

• •

I'm whacking away at these proposals—both *Place* and *Expeditions*—with a pillow when what I need is a scalpel: great wads of material, in which somewhere there lies a book I can't cut out.

I'll struggle along with both for a while longer, then put them aside. A solution to one or the other of them will eventually pop up, or won't, and I will or will not write the book. Or I'll write a proposal, sell it, muddle through the research, come up with a final draft, see it float off into the miracle of production and emerge a book. It'll be assigned a Library of

Congress number, an ISBN number, get listed in this and that, get reviewed. The copies will be packed into cartons, which will be shipped to bookstores. Or to a warehouse somewhere, to languish. I'll struggle to come up with another idea. If this apparently inexorable progression is depressing to me, and it is, imagine how depressing it must be to an editor who sits on six, or ten, or fifty such projects—I have no idea how many—a year.

It's a hell of a thing to be finishing a book in the fall, but I always seem to do it. Autumn, I claim, increases the amplitude of everyone's moods, not just mine. Writing an informal thank-you note, I find myself attempting to cut through to the deepest truths of a relationship, for no reason at all, with someone I barely know. I make some mild gaffe at a social gathering and brood about it for ten days, picking away at it, concocting elaborate explanations to myself for my insensitivity. (It is time, says C., for me to stop going to parties for a while.) A certain quaver comes into my correspondence, and my conversation. I'd hate this time of year if it weren't so beautiful, if I didn't enjoy it so much. Amazing time to try to finish a book. Sometime I should try wrapping one up in the spring.

• •

Yesterday afternoon I noticed—for the first time, really—the scarred roots that cross the loop path. The "bark" is worn off, leaving the interior wood exposed, polished by wear. We think of roots as tough, but limbs in the path don't get this scarring; roots do. What's the difference? I wondered if roots even need bark, as such. Roots are in the ground, damp; the covering must stay softened, unable to harden off into a tough coating: more like skin than bark, a bag to contain the moisture rather than a protection against trauma. With no built-up toughness, exposed roots scar very easily. They suffer damaging wear from no more passing traffic than the dogs and me.

This pipsqueak insight is surely a kind of Thoreauvian over-interpretation, perhaps none of it correct, only a writer's imagination at work. It interests me not for what it has to do with roots but for where it came from: a kind of empathy. For some reason I began thinking about the root under the ground, imagining what that would be like, what the root might need. I wouldn't claim to be able to experience "rootness," exactly, but I did find it the only way to think about the question.

C. is much better at this than I. She keeps track of each nesting in our bluebird boxes, so she knows when to expect the hatch and when the fledglings will fly. This requires a considerable investment of what I find not very entertaining time, particularly when the babies are due to leave the nest. She sits quietly, watching with field glasses, in a way I can't manage. I think it is because she puts her attention down in that sweaty little box with the babies, yearning to escape. I can't hang on to that deep empathy.

The trick in observing nature must always be to make that imaginative leap. Needs practice, obviously. I haven't spent enough time at it. I haven't even spent enough time outdoors. Next week will mark our tenth anniversary on this place, but I still haven't been walking the loop long enough; I don't know how to see it yet.

. .

Bernard Malamud is asked how many drafts he does of a novel: "Many more than I call three. Usually the last of the first puts it in place. The second focuses, develops, subtilizes.

By the third most of the dross is gone. I work with language.
I love the flowers of afterthought."

He is asked, "Your style has always seemed so individual,
so recognizable. Is this a natural gift, or is it contrived and
honed?"

Malamud: "My style flows from the fingers. The eye and
ear approve or amend."

*A well-known writer got collared by a university student who
asked, "Do you think I could be a writer?"*
*"Well," the writer said, "I don't know. . . . Do you like
sentences?"*
                                    —Annie Dillard, *The Writing Life*

DECEMBER

· ·

*P*aris Review interview with Carlos Fuentes:
"In a way we are all involved in the
same adventure: to know what you are
going to say, to have control over your material, and at
the same time to have that margin of freedom which is discovery, amazement, and a precondition of the freedom of the
reader."

··

Gray, bitterly cold, three above zero at dawn. I'm getting
frustrated over how little I'll actually be able to get into a
proposal for *Expeditions*. A book proposal has to be pulled
tight enough so the prospective editor can quickly understand
what it's about. That means finding a way to make it attractive
without taking the time to demonstrate the richness of the
subject. Georges advises that proposals be kept to ten to twelve
pages, because people in the business simply have too much
to read. I'm sure he's right, but someday I'd like to go the

other way and do a sixty-pager. Maybe *Expeditions* is the one to try it with.

• •

Liz Libbey—an accomplished poet and teacher, as well as Willy's wife—has inherited the journals, correspondence, and surveying tools of a great-grandfather named Milton Ensign, and wants to dig a book out of them. C. had lunch with her yesterday, and volunteered to help her get started doing research, at which she hasn't much experience. When C. told me this, it got me thinking about what I would say to someone starting a book, which quickly turned, in my head, into a discussion of working method—ostensibly for Liz but in fact for myself, for any new project. I believe I'll write Liz a letter about this, just to get it down on paper. As a reminder to myself.

• •

Ran errands yesterday, and, driving around the valley, began another of my patented late-autumn descents into gloom—most of it rubbing off from the Christmas decorations. Later I realized once again that if I'd been a spectator rather than an actor, if I had looked at the crowded roads and the holiday merchandising crap as things to write about, then I might have gotten interested. I could have enjoyed it.

But there is always the tainting factor. *Stone Work* opens with a scene of the dogs chasing Frisbees in a spring snowstorm. I remember that day well, how beautiful the sight was, and how as soon as I realized that, I also realized that I would eventually write about it. At that moment I started losing it: spoiling it, overinterpreting it, searching for the words to put on it instead of just taking it in, getting it as it was. I suppose this is the writer's dilemma. I'd prefer to have been there, completely in the present tense, getting it at the time. Failing that—as I always fail to acquire the present-tense experience —I'd rather have it reconstructed, I guess, than to have let it slip away completely.

There seems to be a certain miserly hoarding of experience going on here.

$$\cdot \cdot$$

C.'s contract arrived and she has signed it, with some nervousness, never having entered into that kind of legal obligation to produce work before. Her agent won most of the battles, but had to surrender the option on her next work.

Publishers look at the option clause as a way of protecting their investment in the writer. Writers—this writer, anyway —look at it as a reserve clause, a device for preventing us from improving our lot. Fetching a sample from my collection of old contracts, I see that in the more or less typical option clause the publisher wasn't required to respond to a next proposal from me until thirty days after publication of the work under the contract. That meant I couldn't get a decision on whether my next book project was acceptable, and couldn't legally submit it to any other publisher, until about nine months after finishing the book on hand. Thus I couldn't effectively generate any more book income for that length of time.

Georges has been effective at protecting me from that kind of legal handcuff in recent years, but there are plenty of other impediments to writers' solvency in the way publishing does business. Assume for a moment that the book under that contract had been a huge smash, earning a million dollars. Publishers pay royalties six months after each reporting period. If the book was finished in March and published in January, the next reporting period would likely close the following March, so the first royalty check would be issued in August—eighteen months after I'd turned in the book and received the last payment on its advance, twenty-seven months after I'd have been allowed to generate some other kind of book income. Of course with a smash, I could probably have borrowed against royalty to come, but living in debt is not a productive way to generate good new work.

One suspects that publishers would prefer that writers not live entirely off book projects, but supplement their income with teaching or journalism or some other form of taking in laundry. That way we wouldn't need such large advances. One even suspects that publishers would prefer we become movie stars, politicians, sports heroes, or titans of industry. Publishers know how to sell books by those types better than they do books written by writers.

• •

For some reason *Place* is on my mind again this morning. Maybe the proposal is ready for another run-through. If I could write a coherent statement of what the book is really about, it might be ready to test in the market.

I keep telling myself that it is about how place shapes lives, but I've never really faced up to saying what that means. I need to talk about how, for instance, twelve inches of annual rainfall makes one understand the natural world differently than sixty inches does. How do the simple physical facts influence what you think is possible in the world you're living in? What conservatisms come into your thinking when you live in an area that gets temperatures of thirty-five below zero—or a hundred and twelve above? How much does physical geography determine whether you see the natural world as a hostile or a forgiving place? What's the difference when you grow up in a world of wide-brimmed hats and dark glasses as compared with earmuffs and long underwear? Do you automatically dance out of the way when you turn over a rock, afraid of scorpions or snakes? Are you willing to walk off into a weed patch, unsure what combination of thorns and stickers and fangs and poisons you're likely to encounter? Is nature hard or soft to you? Is a breeze a blessing or a curse? Which indigenous plants make you feel at home, and which speak of foreignness?

In Europe and in Japan I've tried to see the landforms and vegetation as somehow different, to see the natural world itself as foreign. I fail; the architecture, cuisine, and language may be foreign but the landforms and vegetation, even the wildlife, are more or less familiar. The earth is the earth, and there are only so many things nature chooses to do with rock and water and earth and wind.

But it isn't the big stuff that determines the genius of place; that, too, has to be in the details. I don't know, maybe the book would finally find that, for example, a certain laconic native wit is universal. The rural West Texan and the rural New Englander have different accents and different vocabularies for saying pretty much the same things, for making the same wry, rock-bottom observations. They have the same understanding of how things operate in the physical world, no matter how the conditions vary—and the same mystification at the way we complicate them in our urban gatherings. They are equally offended, or bewildered, by urban complications —just as urban people are offended by the hard-bitten realities of rural life.

Leaving the land does seem a key to the book. The unfortunate truth seems to be that the ones who stay and try to make a place work are usually the less ambitious, less energetic, at least in the media sense of these terms. Maybe more energy is required to stay and make things work than to leave the land. Perhaps the book is trying to be about the tension between those who leave and those who stay.

This is empty rhetoric. I still don't know how I'm going to write a wider book. Don't know how to write this book at all, just know how to write the personal memoir. Even if I can get a broader approach to cohere, the book that I want to write is my own response to place, my personal vision and understanding, and that's specifically what robs it of the wide appeal that a publisher is looking for.

So, perhaps I should try to get foundation support for this ego trip? Dubious. I wonder how much time I've put into *Place* so far. Time is the writer's only capital. Freelance writers are like hummingbirds or shrews, I think, functioning on a precariously narrow energy budget—although in the writer's case you can drop the word "energy."

· ·

These book ideas keep spewing out not because I actually dream of writing them, I suspect, but as a form of validation, to prove my existence. Some of the better ideas, at least in my opinion, would have less chance in the marketplace, which is what makes me think of trying the foundations.

Actually, the federal government should pay me a subsidy not to publish. Let me go ahead and have the ideas, enjoy them, just not turn them into manuscripts. I don't make enough now for the Feds to get a decent tax bite. When publishers lose money on me, they deduct those losses from their taxes, further reducing the government's take. We waste trees.

If the government paid me to take my writing machine out of production, everyone would come out ahead. I'd pay taxes on the subsidy, and would no longer get tax breaks for the expense of doing business; the publishing industry would be more profitable and pay more taxes. Publishing would prosper and put more people to work, and the government would collect taxes from them. In addition to the trees, we'd save all that landfill space, all those warehouses no longer needed for storing unsold copies of books.

I'd go on writing, but to please myself, not for the marketplace. With no time pressure, I'd produce better work. If I did, some of it might be profitably publishable, in which case the publisher could buy back my subsidy and get the work cheap.

I keep getting these images of grain elevators throughout the Midwest, filled with old manuscripts. There ought to be other uses for old manuscripts. Insulation? Mulch?

• •

At age fifty-seven I find myself still learning to work. Keeping a journal focused on writing matters has taught me more about how to work than anything else I've ever done. I can't say too emphatically how valuable it is to keep a journal, if for nothing else than as a way of examining one's own working methods, for finding out how you can be more productive— and therefore less frustrated. Others will have to judge what it does for the quality of the work, but for the frustration level, I can verify that it does wonders.

I also learn from watching C. begin work on a book. She has a more systematic mind than I, and goes at things in ways that I have yet to discover. There's another side to that coin, of course: I try to help her organize her project, even if only in dinner-table conversation, and in attempting to teach, I learn.

One of our shared realizations is how rarely you can pose the right questions ahead of time. You have to struggle with the material until an answer comes to the surface, and only then, usually, can you figure out what the questions are. This is why journalistic training (which I lack) must surely help: it makes you keep asking questions early. What have you left out, what isn't told, what does the reader need to know? What's still on your side of the typewriter, that you've simply forgotten to put in? This is why a journalistic editor is valuable. Also irritating.

I prefer a literary editor, of course. Such editors have perfect confidence in their own tastes, and therefore give the writer confidence too, helping him to make leaps he might not otherwise be able to make. The journalistic editor, by contrast, pushes. Both techniques elicit good work, the only difference being the comfort level. There are writers who want an adversarial relationship with the editing process, who find it forces them to produce better work. I am not one of them.

· ·

Dear Liz:

This is to recapitulate our discussion about getting started on a book. As I said, when I found myself writing a letter to you in my head, I realized I wasn't writing to you but to myself, talking myself through the process of getting started on my own next book. I want to get that down on paper. I'd be interested in your reaction.

First advice to myself: I must remember that writing is very easy, just as Mark Twain said. All I have to do is tell the story—whatever the story is—as cleanly and clearly and economically as I can. In the process of doing that, however, it is my obligation to find out everything I possibly can about everything *in* the story, and tell that, too, as cleanly and clearly and economically etc.

Thus for *Place* I have to start by finding out everything I can about Coleman Ward, the Cherokee who ran the tourist court where my father used to take us fishing in the Kiamichi Mountains. I will try to track down his descendants, see if the tourist court still exists, find out who lives now on that particular parcel of land and what happened to the family. Then I want to expand outward from there, investigating, for example, the post-Depression fate of Native American subsistence farmers in southeastern Oklahoma. I'll want to gather and summarize the physical geography of the Kiamichi Mountains. And so on.

Similarly, I'd think you'd simply want to find out and tell the story of Milton Ensign's life. To tell that I assume you'll want to know something about, for example, those early surveying and drafting tools and how they were used. (I use this example because their existence is all I know of Milton.) It would be helpful to find out what daily life was like for a surveyor of his era, what towns he lived in or visited and what they were like at the time, who the influential people in his life were (and what their stories were), and so on—damn near to infinity. Suddenly it is not so easy—but suddenly it is incredibly rich, bursting with possibility, isn't it? Wouldn't it be exciting to come across a dusty old surveyor's plat somewhere with Milton's signature on it?

The reason to find out everything one can is because everything leads on to something else, and some of those things will be truly illuminating. Something about how surveying tools are used might help you understand how Milton Ensign saw the world, how he expressed himself, might help you see why he included the things he did in his diaries—or even what the omissions were. Understanding how he made his living might help you better understand how he thought about the world economically and socially, might even help you understand something about the history of the country that none of us has quite seen before.

In other words, the job is still to make it new (thanks, Ezra). As a writer you have to do this with the same old nouns and verbs, the same sentences, parts of speech, syntactical relationships. Impossible; the only solution, the only possible newness, will come in ideas clearly stated. Ideas breed ideas: every new thing you learn about your subject will cause more ideas to sprout in your head. I guarantee it.

You also may very well be going into this project with no clear notion of what the story is, of what this piece of writing is even about. Not knowing where you are headed will make you fear your story's ordinariness. But ordinariness is only a sign you haven't yet gone deep enough—or that ordinariness itself is your story. That's okay; so is not knowing where you're headed. It is more difficult to maintain headway without a sense of direction to drive you, but you can wait it out with confidence. What the story is will eventually blossom up out of the material (filling you with wonder).

The daunting thing about these projects is that they get so large so fast they scare us off. One trick for controlling the size—and the fright—is to get a narrative of some sort going. That allows you to follow twists and turns, doing just what turns up, thus relieving yourself of the responsibility of covering the history of Western man. The handiest and most serviceable narrative thread is to stick yourself into the book, make it your story too. Someone else's life will work just as

well. The great thing about following a narrative thread anywhere it takes you is that you can't get lost. What interests you
in finding out the story is what is going to interest the
reader—if you can tell it clearly enough.

I just ran across a discussion of this in *Information Anxiety*,
by Richard Saul Wurman:

> You can follow any interest on a path through all knowl-
> edge. Interest connections form the singular path to
> learning. It doesn't matter what path you choose or
> where you begin the journey. A person can be interested
> in horses, or automobiles, or color, or grass, or the con-
> cept of time, and, without forcing the issue whatsoever,
> can make connections to other bodies of information.
> . . . The trick is to separate that which you are really
> interested in from that which you think you should be
> interested in. The pursuit of the first will provide plea-
> sure; the pursuit of the second will produce anxiety. . . .
> The concept of interest may be simple-minded, but I
> believe that because of this, it should be a word of special
> delight, because it represents a way to get in touch with
> clarity.

I particularly like that word "clarity."

There are some other tricks for reducing the frightful size
of the project. My favorite is to divide the project into five
files, five categories of information that are critical to the project, and then to start filling up those files. Then no matter
what screwball aspect of the thing I happen to come across,
I can toss it into the appropriate hopper, or what seems at
the moment to be the appropriate hopper. It doesn't matter
much what the five categories are (see Wurman's horses, automobiles, color, grass, time). Anything will do for starters;

the categories get revised as my grip on the project becomes more secure.

Of course the number five is arbitrary also—that's just the number I usually come up with. Wurman, incidentally, says that there are only five ways of organizing information (category, time, location, alphabet, or continuum, by which he means ordering by size, price, weight, or some other rankable characteristic). I don't know if he's right about the number five, I'm just looking for someplace to put things until I can get back to them more attentively. Five seems the most useful number I can get my mind around. I'm speaking of computer files, which do make this approach faster, but computers aren't necessary: cardboard file folders—or shoe boxes—will do as well.

The five-category approach is important to me because it's the key to the only writing secret I know, the only concrete tip I have to offer. Once I've begun to get material dumped into separate files, I am never again at a loss for how to proceed—and relieving that particular anxiety is, I think, the secret to happiness at the writing machine. Whenever I get back to the project, I just pull out a file and start writing my notes. That is, I pick a category and start organizing the notes that are in it: I start to *write* them, to polish them, to rewrite them, to try to say them more effectively. I try to turn them into nice little pieces of writing ahead of time, before I know where they go in the story, before I even know if they are useful.

The ostensible reason is so I will only need to paste them in place later. That, however, is only to convince myself to keep working at them; the real reason for doing it is that working through them, again and again, develops the whole project. The process points out ways to go, ways of treating the material, that I wouldn't otherwise discover. Rewriting the notes literally shapes the piece: I begin to learn the specific language that is required for this piece of writing, learn how to talk about its subject matters, get fluent in my own subject. Holes in the research become evident. Narrative threads emerge: story lines, approaches, ways of saying things. This rewriting of notes is, I think, the single most important thing I've learned about writing this year.

The only other thing that's necessary, I think, is learning to make better sentences. The struggle always seems to be about getting the rhythm right, making the sentences more graceful, giving them some balance. But the way you get the rhythm right is always by finding out what you're trying to say.

Grace in a sentence comes from truth, I think, not from rolling syllabification or fancy punctuation, not from ripping off skeins of parallelism or juxtaposing startling or novel ideas. There are sentences that will knock you over with their beauty and balance and internal music, their precision of expression. E. B. White was the master of sentences that stop you dead in your tracks. Unfortunately, stopping sometimes makes you examine them as sentences instead of as ideas.

What you finally arrive at is only *your* truth, the truth for you. When the sentence finally works out, it clicks into place, shining a ray of clarity into the confusion with which you've been struggling. A clear sentence is a moral act. More, it somehow authenticates you. You utter it with total confidence, with a full sense of self. These are the sentences that keep me writing. The possibility of creating them is simply the most interesting task that I have ever tried, that I've ever been able to think of. If every sentence that I write doesn't offer at least that possibility—of expressing my own particular truth—then

248

I am writing about the wrong things. I'm not interested enough. I don't want to work that way. It's too hard, it isn't worth it.

Anyway, if you can hang on to this little schema—tell the story, break down the piece, rewrite your notes—you can write a book from it. It'll get you working and keep you working, I think, until you learn enough about how to write a book for yourself—until you learn how to do what it is you're going to end up doing.

This is what I think Mark Twain meant when he said that writing is very easy, you just cross out the wrong words. You find out everything and get everything down, and then just cross out the things that don't fit: the things that distract or mislead or confuse, that get in the way of the telling of the story straight. In other words, selection is all. It is in selecting what to include and what to leave out that art comes in.

End of How-to-Write-a-Book: The Essay. (No need to wait for the movie.) I should also say that there's a lot of bullshit throughout the above, particularly at those places where I used the word "easy." It is never easy—but little pieces of it sometimes are. One of my motives for bouncing this off you is that I hope you will help me figure out what is bullshit, what is unhelpful. What if any *is* helpful, and might be expanded.

One last joke. I mentioned at lunch that marvelous line in Dillard's *The Writing Life*: "I don't know, do you like sentences?" I'd never have had the wit to give an answer like that, I'm not that quick, but if anyone ever does ask me the question, I am now ready for it. Forget sentences, I'm going to quote Susan Sontag: "The writer's volume of accomplishment depends precisely on the ability to sit alone in a room." If someone ever asks me if he or she could become a writer, that's what I intend to say: I don't know, how do you like sitting alone in a room?

Love,

. .

After subtracting the copies returned by bookstores, *Stone Work* seems to have sold not eight thousand but sixty-three hundred copies. Oh well. The reviews, if not the sales, have been beyond my wildest dreams. Similarly the New Hampshire piece, at least from the professional publishing people who have seen it (it's scheduled for February): last week Todd held it up to another writer as a model for writing about place.

So. This year I wrote a *Runner's Log*, a book review, a magazine feature, some miscellaneous other short bits, and the first draft of this manuscript. Sold X words for Y dollars; end-of-year bank balance: $1,738.99. (But I owe the IRS $1,600 of that. Clerical error.) I am owed a few dollars. It'll work out.

I write this on December 28, on a bright, clear, pretty morning after a below-zero night, having survived another Christmas. Spent the early hours cleaning up the letter to Liz, then brought this page up to date, and looked around for the next thing to do, and there isn't one. I grind to a stop, caught up. Think I'll take the rest of the year off.

. .

I head out on the loop, shuffling on snowshoes across firm snow a foot deep. Snowshoes turn the entire hillside into trail, allowing me to roam anywhere; whenever my eye sees any interesting thing, I just walk right over to it. The snow also smooths the woods' fuzziness, drawing hard-edged outlines everywhere, erasing the vegetative vagueness of summer and fall. I am struck by the snow's apparent solidity. But snowshoes

250

are awkward on a slant, reminding me that the hillside is a tilted plane, a ramp loaded with unimaginable tons of water. All that energy poised above the house would be frightening if autumn hadn't first put down such a nice layer of glue between hillside and snow: all the dead leaves, sopped into place with the fall rains, functioning as a kind of natural Velcro. The snow even puts stoppers in the erosional sluiceways, those dark arrows where fall rains washed the leaves away. Snow locks the entire hillside in place. It's winter, dammit, says the snow; slow down.

Snowshoes achieve the same effect with me. They also spread my weight across the snow so I don't sink in, making my presence intrude less on the hillside. Maybe this empathy practice is paying off: I may yet succeed in becoming, in my imagination, the hill. Maybe I'm acquiring the habit.

I've been trying. The other morning, attempting to hone those skills, I lay abed imagining a sentient world. I felt the blanket covering us and tried to become that blanket in my mind, feeling for a moment the lift and fall, the subtle updraft of warmth and water vapor from the sleeping bodies beneath me. I tried experiencing mattress-ness—a bit of a stretch, frankly—then became, in my imagination, the bed itself, the bed frame, accepting the weight in the center of me, splaying my four legs micrometrically to take a larger stance on the floor of the bedroom. I worked my way downward, turning myself into the floor, the basement, the house itself, finally becoming the earth accepting the weight of the house, feeling the tiny weight shift as occupants walk from room to room. It's an interesting exercise.

Now I try to become the hillside as I walk it, feeling these puny little biped footsteps tickle my surface. I try to become the chilly wind, whipping around cold tree trunks as well as warm pedestrians, flowing over the surface of the snow, sucked down into shady cold hollows, bounced upward again by reflecting heat. The sun gets my attention as my shadow interrupts its rays on their way to the surface of the hill; I turn to the west just as it is setting, and almost feel myself spinning backward, away from its light. Feel the earth and me on it, the hemisphere and my hillside spinning backward into the night. Almost, almost.

So I try, for a moment, to become the sun—an act of anthropomorphism so breathtakingly arrogant that it makes me grin. If I were the sun I would be sweetly entertained, I think, by the play of my light across hillside and dark trees, limbs and faces of creatures, on the side of the globe that I happened to be illuminating at the moment. What a glittering ball the earth must be from that point of view: surfaces changing, reflections bouncing and glaring and refracting off into the distance. If the sun were sentient, it would have to enjoy that, wouldn't it? The sight of its own light shining on the earth, on us? The sun must enjoy shining; you can almost feel that, on a December afternoon, when you turn your face to its warmth.

Well. Winter has its highs as well as lows. As I shuffle on, I amuse (and reassure) myself by thinking how the snow shifts the erosional processes to a finer level, its product now seeping molecules, in place of earlier autumn's tumbling chunks and particles. Velocity sorts by size; a stream slows and drops a sandbar on the inside of every bend, speeds up on the outside—the differential effect, like a car's rear axle—and carves away the outer bank. It is such a pleasure to walk along thinking about the way real things work, the physics of things. It allows me to step out of the buzz, out of the culture for a while. How restful that is. The natural world is so much more

interesting than anything else. If I could just turn my proper
attention to it, I wouldn't have time to write. I'd stop writing.
(Achieve my mantra! Get out of my head and into . . . *It! Be*
the hillside, let wild things play on my flanks! This has
possibilities.)

Can't do it. Can't keep my mind on it without writing it
down. Can't stop writing. That's okay. We're past the solstice.
The sun's coming back. I have this wonderful deal.

· ·

I spent the next year rewriting this journal into the book you now hold. Things happened during that process that shed new light on the year I was attempting to document, and I was tempted several times to move one year's experiences into the previous one, but didn't. This is pretty much how it happened.

The New Hampshire piece ran in the February issue of *New England Monthly* as the cover story, and received as gratifying a reaction—from my peers—as any magazine piece I've ever done. Not, however, from the public. The cover photo was a sunset shot of Kinsman, pink-tinged, looming over Ion and Peg Whitcomb's barn; I thought it was beautiful, but magazine readers seem not to have: February turned out to be the worst-selling issue in history. I don't *think* I started the downslide, but *NEM* folded seven months later, spewing a splendid crop of writers and editors into the marketplace. It was a fine publication that couldn't survive in a postliterate economy. There is a sentiment in the media business that the magazine is a dead form.

Despite that dim outlook, Dan Okrent has already become a magazine doctor, consulting on other people's new ventures while he waits for just the right book to develop for him to write. Dick Todd continues developing new authors and helping the old ones produce good books for Houghton Mifflin; he's also begun doing more freelance writing. I wish he'd write a book, about anything. I'd like to read it. After a long search for research support, Bill MacLeish has plunged ahead with his next book. Liz Libbey, now teaching full time, has finished a new volume of poetry, and continues to circle her Milton Ensign material warily. Hans Teensma has designed several new magazines, and his studio flourishes; Lynne Bertrand has sold one children's book and has several other irons in the fire, including a new baby on the way. Mary Priscilla Howes died suddenly, devastating the townspeople of Ashfield.

C.'s book—working title, *The Cruise of the Sairy Gamp*—took us canoeing. We spent three days on the water in the Adirondacks in May, six days in Ontario in July, then twenty-eight days in the Adirondacks in August and September, the last trip a hundred and eighty miles long, twenty-eight days outside the buzz. That alone would have been worth becoming a writer for. She is writing a wonderful book.

Both the *Place* and *Expeditions* proposals were dropped; before either came clear I had a better idea. I started walking the loop twice a day. The dogs love it, and my productivity has increased to match.